功能译论下的
广告翻译研究

**Advertising Translation Between English and
Chinese from Functionalist Perspective**

董岩　著

中国海洋大学出版社
·青岛·

图书在版编目 (CIP) 数据

功能译论下的广告翻译研究 / 董岩著 . -- 青岛：
中国海洋大学出版社, 2024.1
　ISBN 978-7-5670-3603-1

　Ⅰ . ①功… Ⅱ . ①董… Ⅲ . ①广告—翻译—研究
Ⅳ . ① F713.8

中国国家版本馆 CIP 数据核字 (2023) 第 170109 号

出版发行	中国海洋大学出版社	
社　　址	青岛市香港东路 23 号　　**邮政编码**　266071	
出 版 人	刘文菁	
网　　址	http://pub.ouc.edu.cn	
电子信箱	184385208@qq.com	
责任编辑	付绍瑜　　　　　　　　　**电　　话**　0532-85902533	
印　　制	山东彩峰印刷股份有限公司	
版　　次	2024 年 1 月第 1 版	
印　　次	2024 年 1 月第 1 次印刷	
成品尺寸	148 mm×210 mm	
印　　张	4.25	
字　　数	105 千	
印　　数	1 ～ 1000	
定　　价	46.00 元	
订购电话	0532-82032573（传真）	

如发现印装质量问题 , 请致电 13053687153, 由印刷厂负责调换。

前言 / PREFACE

In modern society, advertising is becoming an increasingly important part of our daily life. The intensification of international exchanges and the severe competition involves a growing need for advertising and thus of its translation. As a branch of translation study, advertising translation, different from literary translation, has its own intrinsic laws and demands a systematic study.

As a practical type of writing, advertising aims to persuade consumers or the public to accept the products, services or ideas advertised and to take immediate action. An advertisement which fails to lure consumers into buying is undoubtedly a great failure. The same is true with the translated advertising text. Therefore, the study of advertising translation must incorporate the special purpose and function of advertising with translation theories. The widely accepted and highly praised equivalence-based theories, such as Yan Fu's principle of "faithfulness, expressiveness and elegance" and Nida's equivalence theory, however, seem increasingly inadequate when guiding advertising translation for their confinement to verbal transfer only, stress on the equivalence between the target text (TT) and the source text (ST) and negligence of the realization of the intended function of the TT in target culture (TC) .

As a break with the traditional translation ideas and an important complement to translation studies, the functionalist concept put forward by some German scholars has opened up a new perspective for the study of advertising translation. The two general rules as well as backbones of the approach are the skopos rule and the loyalty rule. The skopos rule is the core which holds that the skopos or the intended function of the TT determines the whole translation process including the option of translation strategies and methods. The loyalty rule means that the translator has moral responsibility for the source-text producer and the target-text receiver. Besides, there are two secondary rules: coherence rule (intratextual coherence) and fidelity rule (intertextual coherence). The four rules are not of equal importance. The skopos rule and the loyalty rule can be applied in any translation process, but the coherence rule and the fidelity rule work only in special cases. The fidelity rule is subordinated to the coherence rule and both are subordinated to the skopos rule and the loyalty rule. The functionalist approach to translation shares much with advertising: its stress on the realization of the intended function of the TT and thus the agent role of the receiver and other contextual factors is in tune with the stylistic characteristics and function of advertising text; with the introduction of the concept of translational action, it brings into the domain of translation study the transfer of non-verbal signs which are becoming increasingly important in international advertising; its dethronement of the ST happens to accord with the target-audience orientation of advertising; the crucial role it entrusts on the translator is in line with that of the advertising-maker; it provides a sound theoretical basis for some unconventional translation methods such as addition, abridgement, rewriting which have proved to be effective in advertising translation; vocative text, such as advertisement, deserves functional translation.

Generally speaking, there exist two translation strategies: source-language-culture-oriented strategy and target-language-culture-oriented strategy. The frequently seen translation methods include transliteration, literal translation, free translation, adaptation and rewriting, etc. Due to the great linguistic and cultural differences of English and Chinese ads, an ad with positive effect in source culture (SC) may encounter Zero or even negative effect if translated absolutely equivalently. The author conducts a small-scaled questionnaire on the popularity of the translated ads among target audiences and draws a conclusion that advertising translation should take the target-language-culture-oriented strategy, with the advertising function of TT taken into account. The competent advertising translators also adopt this strategy, consciously or unconsciously, in real-life. In addition, the emphasis on the intended function of TT by functionalist theories coincides with the peculiarities of advertising. Therefore, this book proposes that advertising translation should take the target-language-culture-oriented strategy and make full and flexible use of all translation techniques including those conventional such as transliteration, literal translation, and those unconventional, such as addition, deletion, rewriting, so as to fulfill the intended purpose or function of the TT to its best.

Like many theories, functionalist approach to advertising translation is not perfect. It may inevitably cause loss in form and meaning to some degree and thus belittlement of the advertising effect and persuasive function while attempting to achieve functional adequacy because of the linguistic and cultural differences, which is the limits of translatability in advertising translation. With the deepening of international interaction, the problem will be solved little by little.

目 录 CONTENTS

Chapter 1　Introduction

　　Advertising, according to the American Marketing Association, is defined as "the non-personal communication of information usually paid for and usually persuasive in nature about products, services or ideas by identified sponsors through the various media." (Ding & Kang, 2019: 1) The feature of pervasiveness of advertising in contemporary society is undeniable: whether it is loved, hated or just ignored, its presence is a defining feature of modern culture. Whenever we turn on a radio or a TV, we may see or hear advertisements; whenever we read a newspaper or a magazine, we may encounter advertisements; whenever we walk on the street, we are sure to be faced with advertisements on billboards or buildings; and even when we take a bus or a tube, we are confronted with advertisements. It is no exaggeration to say that there are few places in the public that are not permeated with advertisements, the embodiment of commerce. Advertising has become an essential part of our life, for it is playing an inestimable role in promoting the development of national economy and flourishing the market.

Advertising is not new; it can be traced to as early as 3,000 BC when the first advertisements were discovered for an ointment dealer, a scribe and a shoemaker on Babylonian clay tablets. However, the advertising industry in China is comparatively young. The history of organized advertising in China dates back to the late 1970s when the policy of Reform and Opening-up policy was carried out, though it traces back to the mid-17th century in the west. Nevertheless, advertising is a fast growing industry in China today.

With the rapid development of China's economy and the enforcement of the policy of Reform and Opening-up policy, as well as China's entry into WTO, more and more Chinese products are exported to foreign countries, and in the meantime, countless foreign goods and services are flooding into Chinese market. The intensification of international exchanges and severe competition involve a growing need for advertising and thus of its translation. International advertising has become a very specialized field of translation practice in modern societies.

However, the study of advertising translation, especially that between English and Chinese, is far from satisfactory to its need either in quantity or in quality, either at home or abroad. Advertising translation was mentioned in translation studies for the first time in Hurbin's (1972) article "Peut-on Traduire la Langue de la Publicite" ('Can one translate the language of advertising?'). Hurbin's article appeared in a period when linguistic study of translation was primarily concerned with the notion of equivalence. In the 1960s and 1970s, there were many publications focusing on equivalence put forward by Nida, Taber and Catford, etc. Hurbin points out that there are a number of translations for any original text; it is the translator's task to choose the most appropriate of these possibilities. This is easier if glossaries of advertising language based on specific product categories are compiled so that when translating, the most appropriate equivalents are found. Although there are merits to this method, for patterns do exist in advertising for certain products, the use of standard glossaries does not take into account the creativity of advertising. During the following 20 years, there was a shift in the focus of translation studies. Equivalence was no longer the major concern of translation studies, as functionalism had taken the centre stage. Seguinot (1995), in her article "Translation and Advertising: Going Global" published in Schaffner & Kelly-Holmes' *Cultural Functions of Translation*, highlights firstly what changes globalization has brought to translator's role. But her conclusions are mainly drawn upon somewhat subjective reasoning rather than empirical study. Besides, she regards culture-specific issues as one of the most problematic aspects of translation for a globalized market, but she fails to provide a profound analysis and a satisfying approach to the problem. Another representative paper was Smith & Klein-Braley's (1997) "Advertising: A Five-stage Strategy for Translation" published in *Translation as Intercultural Communication* edited by Nord et al. Based on contrastive analysis of English and German advertisement examples, Smith & Klein-Braley develop a taxonomy of strategies for the analysis of translated advertisements. Their comparison of paired translations proves a useful tool for analysis and the proposed categorization is somewhat meaningful. But their findings may be hard to generalize since they have only used a very small sample (only six pairs). Furthermore, it should not be applied as a framework to the analysis of Chinese and English advertisements without adjustment. Since mid-1990s, studies carried out in the translation of advertising materials have increased in line with the emergence of global markets. However, Mathieu Guidere's book *Translating Ads* (2000) is perhaps the only published book exclusively on advertisement translation up to now. The newly published book aims at describing the interactions between advertising and translation at the time of globalism. For Guidere, translators should be aiming at an "effective" text which sells the advertised product or service in the TC. Guidere believes, however, that there should still be some kind of equivalence between the source and target text. According to Guidere, the equivalence does not occur at lexical level. His understanding of equivalence does not necessarily mean fidelity to the ST, since the emphasis is not on staying close to the text, but on the advertisement's ability to communicate meaning and create the necessary effects on the target audience. One of the ways of assessing this effectiveness is to carry out analysis at three levels: semantic, communicative and rhetorical. However, the reader is left dissatisfied. A major question remains unanswered: how can the effectiveness of advertising translation be evaluated? The author only gives a partial answer; he eliminates the question from his field of speculation, supposing that it does not concern the translator. It seems that there is another question for discussion: If the increase in sales is the only criterion to evaluate the effectiveness of advertising translation, how much room is given to the translator?

Domestically, advertising translation didn't emerge as a topical problem and begin to catch Chinese scholar's attention until early 1990s when it still appeared rather primitive along with the then premature advertising proper. An increasing number of academic papers concerning the topic occupy some pages of the major journals on translation studies and some postgraduates began to explore it in their dissertations. Yet, there has never been a single book wholly devoted to this project in China as far as I know. Generally, the papers on advertising translation fall into four groups:

(i) Specific translation skills and methods. This type of papers, limited to piling of several specific translation skills, remains scattered, superficial and unsystematic, though instructive to some degree. Take for example, the papers by Du Shuangshuang (2020), Yang Shifen (2020). (ii) Pragmatic perspective. Such papers as those by Zhu Xiaohua(2017), Wang Jinjin(2018), focusing on the study of equivalent pragmatic effect, are actually hovering around the equivalence-based approaches. (iii) Equivalence-based linguistic approaches. This school, of the greatest number, usually takes the theories of equivalence or equivalent effect proposed by Nida, Newmark as their theoretical basis of advertising translation, such as the studies by Liu Xiao & Liu Zhuyan (2018), Zhao Hui (2020). Their studies, undoubtedly, contribute much to the study of advertising translation but still have defects which will be elaborated in the following paragraph. (iv) German functionalist approaches. This group is of comparatively least proportion, such as the papers by Zhang Dongdong (2020), Xu Tingting (2021). Their studies have paved a new way for advertising translation and proved effective and significant for the practice as well as the studies of advertising translation. However, most of their pages turn to comparative analysis of linguistic and cultural characteristics and list of specific translation techniques at a microscopic level. So far, it is clear that most of the previous studies on advertising translation were conducted from the angle of traditional equivalence-based linguistic approaches. Even for the few from functionalist perspective, there is still much room for improvement.

However, the traditional equivalence-based approach has defects to advertising translation. (i) The approach confines translation to the verbal transfer only, excluding from the field of translation study of the non-verbal signs which prove to be an increasingly important and even indispensable constituent in international advertising. (ii) It is impossible to achieve absolute equivalent effect or response due to the great differences in languages especially those of different language families such as Chinese and English and communicative context. Newmark (2001: 55) himself admits that there are some cases where the same effect cannot be realized. Snell-Hornby (2001: 22) argues that equivalence-based theories rest on a shaky basis: it presupposes a degree of symmetry between languages which makes the postulated equivalence possible. Moreover, the equivalent effect could not be measured objectively (Munday, 2001: 43). (iii) The approach neglects the fact that some translations function as independent texts in the target culture. In reality, some products are completely foreign-oriented, so the ST does not function as an advertisement in the SC. It is only one of the various sources of information provided to the translator. (iv) The approach excludes many unconventional translation methods such as adaptation, rewriting, addition and abridgement which prove to be effective in translation practice, especially in advertising translation.

But unfortunately, in real-life practice, many people still conduct advertising translation under the guidance of traditional equivalence-based theories which have proved to be increasingly inadequate in that it is more prone to cause bafflement and difficulty in understanding or even ignorance of the goods and services advertised among the target audiences. Very often we can "appreciate" hundreds of translation blunders in advertising. For example, a hair products company, Clairol, introduced the "Mist Stick", a curling iron, into Germany only to find that "mist" is slang for "manure". It is hard to imagine that buyers would like to use the manure stick. In China, most advertisers prefer to use some set phrases to build up the image of their companies and to present the good quality of their products, such as "省优部优" (honored as superior quality product by the provincial government and the Ministry concerned); "在有关部门的领导下，取得了很大进步" (Great improvement has beenmade under the leadership of the sectors concerned). Translations in the above examples do conform to the principle of "faithfulness" in light of traditional equivalence-based translation theories but may be valueless in Western countries because of different cultural norms and thinking patterns. The inadequacy of translation is often caused by inappropriate translation strategies adopted by the translators under inappropriate guiding of principles. A number of academic papers (Wang Xiaoqiong, 2020; Wu Yuedi, 2020; Liu Shuai & Wang Dantong, 2021) has been published criticizing such a negative phenomenon, but so far none has ever adequately described the practice of advertising translation or established a satisfactory model. That's to say, study on advertising translation is far from enough and perfect. It is still an under-explored field which has its own laws and demands a more systematic study on a large scale. Under such circumstances, a more appropriate theoretical framework is called for.

Given the special nature of advertising in style, purpose or function, which differs greatly from literary texts, the present study proposes German functionalist translation theory for the theoretical basis and maintains that it is the most appropriate and applicable theory for guiding advertising translation up till now. Therefore, the book attempts to deeply explore the application of functionalist approach in advertising translation, to provide tentatively the basic strategies of translating advertisements and at the same time to analyze the limits of translatability in advertising translation, thus offering a contribution to the area of the advertising translation between English and Chinese. It aims at bridging the gap between the abundant practice and a not-yet-adequately-researched discipline of advertising translation. This study proceeds to apply the functionalist approach to advertising translation just in order to promote the effective communication of thoughts carried by the advertisements scripts and the conversion between languages.

This book adopts the qualitative and quantitative analysis, but focuses primarily on the qualitative analysis and uses the method of demonstration as its basis. The quantitative analysis takes the form of questionnaire on the popularity of translated advertising texts in target culture in order to find out the preferred translation by the target audience, with the respondents of certain number of Chinese and people from English-speaking countries of different age, occupation and education. The conclusion is based on an objective analysis and calculation of the probability.

Owing to the limited time, space and research conditions as well as the author's limited knowledge in advertising-making, the present research is confined mainly to the commercial advertisements and the transfer of verbal signs of advertising, with the non-commercial advertisements and the transfer of non-verbal signs excluded from its domain.

The significance of the present study lies in both translation theory and practice. (i) While systematic theoretical research on this issue is far from sufficient, translation theorists have not attached special attention to translation of advertisements. Yet, the functionalist theory applied to advertisement serves as a break with the traditional idea of equivalence and an important complement to translation theories, thus opening up a new perspective to advertising translation studies. (ii) The functional concept of translation has provided theoretical basis for a new assessment criterion of advertising translation and provoked reappraisal of certain seemingly unconventional translation methods such as abridgement and adaptation in advertising translation. (iii) The study on the limits of translatability in advertising translation justifies the truth that no translation theory is omnipotent including functional translation theories and that there exists inevitably the loss of communicative function even when functional adequacy has been achieved to its full.

This book consists of six chapters. Chapter 1 covers the background, the objective, the methodology and delimitation and the significance of the study as well as the literature review. Chapter 2 is a brief survey of advertising text, including the definition, the purpose, function and stylistic features of advertisements. Chapter 3 makes a review of functionalist approach to translation, especially the enlightenment on advertising translation. Chapter 4 discusses the strategies of advertising translation and points out that the translation of advertising texts should be target-language-culture oriented. Chapter 5 analyzes the limits of translatability in advertising translation. The conclusion summarizes the major findings of the research and points out the limitations of the present study as well as some suggestions for the future study.

Chapter 2   A Brief Survey of Advertising

2. 1   Definition of Advertising

The word "advertise" originates from the Latin "advertere", meaning "to make known to the public", or "to attract people's attention". Plenty of experts and scholars have reflected on the meaning of the word in different versions of its use. However different in expressions, the essential messages are the same. The present study is done in light of the definition given by American Marketing Association (AMA)—Advertising is "the non-personal communication of information usually paid for and usually persuasive in nature about products, services or ideas by identified sponsors through the various media." (Ding Junjie & Kang Jin, 2019: 1). Several aspects of this definition deserve further explication. "Non-personal" indicates that advertising is directed to groups of people rather than individuals and the message appears in the mass media, which means there is little opportunity for feedback from the message receiver. Because of this, advertisers often utilize some kind of research to predict how a specific target audience might interpret and respond to a message prior to its distribution. The "paid" aspect refers to the fact that normally the advertiser must purchase time and space for the message. Finally, the "identified" aspect refers to the fact that the media require sponsors to identify themselves, for when a message is considered as an advertisement, the sponsor must be identified.

The definition is more embracing and highlights communication and persuasiveness, which is in line with the objectives of the present study. All in all, advertising is a type of communication between certain sponsors and a certain target audience. It provides information of products to consumers with an aim to persuade them to take action on the one hand, help advertisers to expand market on the other hand.

Different standards may lead to different classification of advertisements. According to their coverage, advertisements fall into international advertisements, national advertisement and local advertisements. In the light of people for whom the advertising is intended, it may be divided into import businessman advertisements, dealer advertisements, wholesaler advertisements, retailer advertisements, consumer advertisements, etc. In accordance with the media, the vehicle of advertising, it may be classified into such categories as press advertisements, television and radio advertisements, outdoor advertisements, transport advertisements, direct-mail advertisements, Point-of-Purchase (POP) advertisements etc. That is the most-frequently-seen and simplest approach and from that dimension the categories remain dynamic in that the number would become larger and larger with the possible introduction of new media. Undoubtedly, there are many other ways for its classification. However categorized, all advertisements fall into two groups, namely commercial and non-commercial advertisements. This book concentrates mainly on the former.

2. 2   Purpose and Functions of Advertising

From the definition of advertising mentioned above, we can learn of the purpose and the main functions of advertising. The ultimate purpose of advertising is to promote sales of various products or to popularize the use of services. Styles of advertisements may vary according to the differences in the method of selling, types of products or target audience, but the primary functions of advertising remain the same: persuading and informing. More specifically, the basic functions of advertising are to present some information about goods, services or ideas to the public, to exert influence on them and thus to persuade them to make choices and at least take some actions, especially to purchase the products or services or accept the ideas.

However, the two functions are not of equal importance. Whatever functions an advertisement could perform, advertising is persuasive in nature just as pointed out by the above definition, so the overriding function of advertising is to persuade or manipulate the potential consumers to buy a product and accept the ideas, values and life style that are associated with the product. The persuasive power of an advertisement is exhibited by verbal and non-verbal elements produced by professional advertising experts. Advertisers present information not for improving consumers' knowledge, but for selling their products. Accordingly, we can say that the persuasiveness is the most important function of advertising, and the other functions are taken for the purpose of exerting the persuasive effect at its best.

In summary, advertising is a very practical type of writing with high commercial value. The ultimate purpose of advertising is to promote sales, and all advertisements contain at least two main functions: to inform and to persuade, of which the informative function is subordinate to persuasive function.

According to "Advertising Translation from Functional Perspective"(Lu Yiyang, 2020), the advertising language has the following functions: (i) information function; (ii) demand-creation function; (iii) persuasive function; (iv) get-action function and (v) good-will establishing function.

Within the framework of functionalist approach, texts have four communicative functions: referential or informative, expressive, appellative or operative plus phatic function. Except for purely phatic expressions or utterances, texts are rarely monofunctional. As a rule, we find hierarchies of functions that can be identified by analyzing verbal or non-verbal function markers. An advertisement is informative because it introduces a new product or service to the readers, including its color, size, usage, etc. In order to achieve the communicative purposes, the advertiser appeals to readers' emotion by making abundant use of adjectives, rhetorical devices, favorable syntactical structures, etc. and often creates an aesthetic effect, so advertisements can be expressive too. The appellative or operative function is the most important one for any advertisement. Direct indicators of this function in advertisements would be features like imperative or interrogative questions. The function may also be achieved indirectly through linguistic devices such as superlatives, adjectives or nouns expressing positive values.

2.3　Components and Type of Advertising Text

The purpose of copywriting is to persuade and remind people to take some action to satisfy a need. Therefore, the famous AIDCA principle summarizes what a successful advertisement must be able to achieve: "1. attract attention; 2. arouse interest; 3. stimulate desire; 4. create conviction; and 5. get action", which is the chain reaction in the desirable advertisements accepting process. The copywriter's five tasks may be fulfilled in different parts of the advertising texts. Here is an example.

(1) 大步的跨越，是技术的变革——清华同方率先推出基于英特尔®915 高速芯片组系列技术平台的全新一代主流产品"翻越 E380"

运行更高速：超线程（HT）技术带来双处理器的工作效率。

系统更稳定：智能温控技术配合全新英特尔®处理器及全新英特尔®915 芯片组，使您安全、稳定大跃进。

读取更流畅：采取了 S-ATA 技术的硬盘比 IDE 硬盘快 30%。

升级更具潜力：内存可升级至双通道 DDR，最大支持 2G，支持 4 个 S-ATA 设备，更具扩展性。

基于英特尔®915 高速芯片组系列技术平台的同方商用

电脑 E380，使您的运算更高效、性能更稳定、升级更具潜能。免费订购咨询 800-810-5888　欢迎网上订购 www. tongfangpc. com.（严琦，2021: 69）

Generally speaking, the basic structure of an advertisement copy (verbal part of an advertisement) comprises headline, bodycopy (the main part of the advertising message, often divided into various sections under subheads), signature (a mention of the brand name, often accompanied by a price tag, trademark, or picture of the brand pack) and slogan. Each part may perform different functions as required in the AIDCA principle. Of these parts the headline and signature are the least dispensable; the other components can be, and often are, omitted. Headline along with illustration and slogan is mainly responsible for the first and second tasks, i. e. attention and interest. In the above example, " 大步的跨越，是技术的变革 " functions as the headline to arouse readers' attention and interest. " 清华同方率先推出基于英特尔 ®915 高速芯片组系列技术平台的全新一代主流产品 ' 翻越 E380'", the sub-headline as well as the signature, works to arouse interest and stimulate desire together with the slogan. " 基于英特尔 ®915 高速芯片组系列技术平台的同方商用电脑 E380, 使您的运算更高效、性能更稳定、升级更具潜能 ", the bodycopy containing certain information normally performs the function of desire and conviction. In example (1), the bodycopy presents the special qualities of the product in four concise and parallel sentences. The last requirement—get action is often fulfilled in the concluding paragraph of the copy. As in the above example, the concluding paragraph, "免费订购咨询 800-810-5888 欢迎网上订购 www. tongfangpc. com." means to provide information about the purchase action.

Text type classifications suggest that all texts can be divided into different categories according to the text's dominant function even though texts are rarely monofunctional.

In Reiss' taxonomy, the text types are categorized according to the dominant communicative function of the source text. An informative text, subject-matter-oriented, instructs; an expressive text, sender-oriented, affects; and an operative text, behavior-oriented, persuades.(1989: 1) Nord expands on Reiss's taxonomy by adding a fourth type. Her typology includes the expressive, referential, appellative and phatic function of texts (Nord, 2001: 37-38). Comparison can be made between all these taxonomies, with Reiss's informative and operative being equivalent to referential and appellative texts respectively in Nord.

According to Reiss's functionalist approach to text typology with translation studies, an advertisement is classified as an operative text, with the focus on the text receiver. In operative texts, such as advertising text, "both content and form are subordinate to the extralinguistic effect that the text is designed to achieve"(Nord, 2001: 38). In other words, an operative text calls readers to respond in a certain way and may require them to call on rich knowledge, either of the text genre or culture in general. Operative texts influence readers by appealing to their sensitivities and hidden desires and encouraging them to do something (as in advertising text). The aim of the operative text is to persuade and any information given is secondary to this function. The success of operative text depends on the readers' experiences. Any approach to the translation of advertising materials has to be flexible enough to allow for a wide range of strategies needed to fulfill this goal.

Chapter 3　Functionalist Approach to Advertising Translation

　　Functionalist approach to translation emerged in 1970s in Germany and was introduced into China around the 1990s. As a general theory of translation, it is criticized and challenged by some scholars for its incompatibility with traditional translation theory. However it has been attracting increasing attention in recent years. In her paper "Advertising Translation Based on Functional Concept of Translation", Lu Yiyang (2020) points out that "the concept has provided theoretical basis for some translation practices used to be considered against the existing criteria of translation methods...such as abridgment and adaptation". Zhang Daozhen (2021) also called for more attention to contemporary translation theories such as functionalist approach to translation. He states in his paper "From Traditional to Modern: On the Concept, Methodology and Tasks of Descriptive Translation Criticism" that "by emphasizing the role played by the receptor, the translator and the cultural factors in the process of translation, the functionalist approach is able to present a dynamic and multi-dimensional perspective on translation criticism...". More other scholars are ready to accept this theory and put it into practice. In this book, the background, the development and the basic concepts are discussed in light of their applicability in advertising translation.

3.1   The Background and the Development of the Theory

Functionalism does not suddenly appear overnight. It has experienced a long period of evolution as any other theories. It has been evolving gradually ever since a very early historical time from implicit to explicit. The 20th century witnessed the prosperous and striking development of translation theory with varied schools vying and co-existing with each other, among which the equivalence-based linguistic approach to translation was the dominant one, most probably for the reason that linguistics was the dominant humanistic discipline of the 1950s and 1960s. By 1970s, although the focus shifted from the word or the phrase to the text as a unit of translation, the fundamental linguistic trend was not broken (Nord, 2001: 7). What all the linguistically oriented schools of translation theory have in common, however, is the central concept of translation equivalence (Snell-Hornby, 2001: 15). Equivalence-based translation theories, focusing on the source text, according to which the features of the ST must be preserved in the TT and the TT must be equivalent to the ST, bear their weaknesses as discussed in the Introduction, among which the fatal one is the great gap between such theories and translation practice in that in practice translators have felt for centuries that the process of translating should involve both procedures: a faithful reproduction of source-text qualities in one situation and an adjustment to the target audience in another (Nord, 2001: 9). However, the traditional equivalence-based translation theories exclude many translational phenomena such as adaptation from the field of translation study and thus can hardly describe some common phenomena in translation study. Therefore, the voice of questioning began to be heard and new theories were called for. This is where functionalist translation theories emerged in 1970s in Germany, which is intended to break away with linguistic translation theories and bridge the gap between theory and practice.

Generally speaking, the development of modern functional translation theories has gone through four stages: (i) Katharina Reiss and her functionalist translation criticism; (ii) Hans J. Vermeer's Skopos theory and its extensions; (iii) Just Holz-Manttari's theory of translational action; (iv)

Christiane Nord and the concept of "function plus loyalty". They are German scholars and accordingly called "German School of functionalist translation".

The functionalist approach to translation was born in Germany as early as in 1971, when it was first suggested by Katharina Reiss in her book *Possibilities and Limitations in Translation Criticism*, a book regarded as the starting point for Reiss to deviate from linguistic approaches to functionalist ones. In the book, she includes the "special purpose for which a translation is made" as an additional category in her model of translation criticism—a category which is to replace the normal criteria of equivalence-based translation critique in those cases where the target text is intended for a purpose different from that of the source text. Reiss's view on translation is rather a blended one. On the one hand, she still sticks to the source-text-centered equivalence theory and thinks that the ideal translation would be one "in which the aim in the TL is equivalence as regards the conceptual content, linguistic form and communicative function of a SL text" which she referred to as "integral communicative performance" (ibid.: 9). On the other hand, Reiss knows that real life presents situations where equivalence is not possible and, in some cases, not even desired. To sum up, Reiss believes that "it goes without saying that all types of translation mentioned may be justified in particular circumstances" (1989: 114).

Hans J. Vermeer, Reiss's student, makes a breakthrough by putting forward his famous Skopostheorie which is regarded as the landmark as well as the core of functionalist approach to translation. Vermeer maintains that linguistics alone could not solve all the problems arising in translation. He puts translation in a broader human context, embedding the theory of translation in a theory of human action or activity. To Vermeer, translation is a type of human action, which is "an intentional, purposeful behavior that takes place in a given situation" (Nord, 2001: 11). "Skopos is a Greek word for 'purpose'. According to Skopostheorie, the theory that applies the notion of Skopos to translation, the prime principle determining any translation process is the purpose (Skopos) of the overall translation action." (ibid.: 27)

Justa Holz Manttari, a Finland-based German professional translator, goes one step further than Vermeer. She avoids using the term "translation" in the strict sense and moves away from the traditional concepts and expectations connected with the word. She prefers to speak of "message transmitters" which consist of textual material combined with other media such as pictures, sounds and body movements. She prefers to use translational action rather than translation. The purpose of translational action is to transfer messages across culture and language barriers by means of message transmitters produced by translators whom she refers to as experts in producing appropriate message transmitters (Zhang

Yun, 2020: 82). Holz Manttari places special emphasis on such three areas as the actional aspects of the translation process, the analysis of the roles of the participants and the situational conditions in which their activities take place (Yu Jing, 2020).

Christiane Nord, a German professor of applied linguistics and translation studies, has made tremendous contribution to the development of functionalist theory. She is the first, among other scholars of functional school, to comprehensively systematize various functionalist approaches and vividly illustrate complicated functionalist theory and terminologies with simple English and rich examples. In early 1990s, Nord furthered and improved functionalist translation theory on the basis of former theories and aiming at the defect of attaching so much importance to Skopos as to almost neglect the source text, Nord introduced into the functionalist approaches the principle of "loyalty" which means "the translator is committed bilaterally to the source text as well as to the target situation, and is responsible for both the ST sender and the TT recipient" (Nord, 2001: 126). For her, functionality is still the most important criterion for translation, but certainly not the only one. There must be some relationship between the TL and SL, the quality and quantity of which are specified by the translation Skopos and provide the criteria for the decision as to which elements of the ST-in-situation can be "preserved" and which may, or must be "adapted" to the target situation. Different from "fidelity" which is a rather technical relationship between two texts, Nord's "loyalty" is a moral principle indispensable in the relationship between human beings, who are partners in a communication process. "Function plus loyalty" is one of the main contributions made by Nord to the development and improvement of German School of functionalist translation theory (Yu Jing, 2020).

3. 2　Functionalist Understanding on Translation and Translational Action

In order to understand thoroughly the concepts of functionalist theories, it is quite essential to make clear some related terminologies at first. Skopos, a Greek word for "purpose", is often employed in Skopostheorie to refer to the purpose or function of the TT. Skopostheorie holds that the prime principle determining any translation process is the purpose (Skopos) of the overall translational action. Aim is defined as the final result an agent intends to achieve by means of an action. Purpose is defined as a provisional stage in the process of attaining an aim. Aim and purpose are thus relative concepts. Function refers to what a text means or is intended to mean from the receiver's point of view, whereas aim is the purpose for which it is needed or supposed to be needed. Intention is conceived as an "aim-oriented plan of action" on the part of both the sender and the receiver, pointing toward an appropriate way of producing or understanding the text. As a general rule, Vermeer considers the teleological concepts aim, purpose, intention and function to be equivalent, subsuming them under the generic concepts of skopos (Nord, 2001: 28). Functionalist approach to translation focuses on the intended function of the TT or any of its parts. Functionalism is a broad term for various theories that approach translation in this way.

3.2.1   Translation and Translational Action

Based on action theory, the functionalist school expounds translation from a new perspective. In his book *A Framework for a General Theory of Translation*, Vermeer considers translation (including interpreting) to be a type of transfer where communicative verbal and non-verbal signs are transferred from one language into another (other types would include the transfer from pictures to music or from a blueprint to a building). Translation is thus also a type of human action which is, according to action theory, intentional, purposeful behavior that takes place in a given situation. Holz-Manttari even avoids using the term "translation" in the strict sense. In her model, translation is defined as "a complex action designed to achieve a particular purpose". The generic term for this phenomenon is "translational action", or "translatorial action", or "intercultural cooperation" whose purpose is to transfer messages across culture and language barriers by means of message transmitters consisting of textual material combined with other media. The concept, first presented in 1981 and published in more elaborate form in 1984, is designed to cover all kinds of intercultural transfer including those which do not involve any source or target texts, based on the principles of action theory. Translation and translational action are somewhat different in that the former, in the narrower sense, always involves the use of some kind of ST, whereas the latter may involve giving advice and perhaps even warning against communicating in the intended way (ibid.: 17). Simply speaking, translational action and translation are two circles with the same centre of intercultural communication but different radius. Nord furthered and improved functional translation theory. She defines translation as "the production of a functional target text maintaining relationship with a given ST that is specified according to the intended or demanded function of the TT (translation skopos). Translation allows a communicative act to take place which because of existing linguistic and cultural barriers would not have been possible without it" (ibid.: 28). Nord's definition actually highlights three points: (i) the translated text does have certain function in

TC; (ii) the translated text should remain some relationship with the original text, the quality and quantity of which are determined by the intended function of the TT; (iii) the objectively existing barriers in language and culture must be broken down through translation. However defined, functionalist scholars reach a common understanding of the essence of translation: every translation is a purposeful, intercultural, interpersonal, communicative and text-processing action.

3.2.2   The Roles of the Participants in Translational Action

The people or agents involved in the interaction have certain functions or roles. These roles are interconnected through a complex network of mutual relations. In addition to the source-text producer (the author of the original text), the translator and the target-text receiver, who are considered as the three participants in translation process by traditional theories, functionalist approach includes the initiator, the commissioner, the target text addressee and the target-text user in the group of participants.

The initiator is the person, group or institution that sets off the translation process and determines its course by providing the translation brief which includes explicit or implicit information on the intended function, the addressees, the time, place, occasion and medium of the intended communication. The commissioner serves the intermediary between the initiator and the translator. The initiator actually needs the TT while the commissioner asks the translator to produce a TT for a particular purpose and addressee.

The translator plays a crucial role in the translation process. It is the translator who shoulders the task of turning a text in one language into text in another language through painstaking work. Without the translator, there would simply no translation at all. In functionalist framework, the translator is ostensibly the expert in translational action and should be responsible both for carrying out the commissioned task and for ensuring the result of the translation process. He/She must be well-equipped in two aspects. At first, he/she must be armed with adequate academic knowledge, not only bilingual but bicultural, and a sensitive mind as well, which is the guarantee for the efficiency of his work. Moreover, he/she must be quite aware of his/her responsibilities as a translator. On the one hand, he must ascertain the communicative purpose of the translation either by negotiating with the client or by his own effort when the client has only a vague or even incorrect idea of what kind of text is needed for the communicative situation in question. Then he/she must try his/her best, on the basis of a carefully analysis of the communicative situation, to work out the answers to the questions such as how to go about the translating job, what strategies and methods to employ and so on, so as to produce a TT with the best realization of the intended function. On the other hand, though allocated freedom in a fairly wide range, he/she has moral responsibility for other participants in the translational action, just as the "function plus loyalty principle" requires. He/She must coordinate with other parties for some specific issues in some cases. So far, it is concluded that the translator, within the functionalist framework, must be knowledgeable, sensitive, initiative, creative and responsible as well and therefore works as a visible entity in the whole translation process, which differs greatly from the traditional equivalence-based theories within which the translator functions as an invisible and passive linguistic converter.

The source-text producer has produced the text that is to serve as the source for a translational action. Nord makes a distinction between the sender and the text producer. The sender of the text is the person, group or institution that uses the text in order to convey a certain message; the text producer is the one actually responsible for any linguistic or stylistic choices present in the text expressing the sender's communicative intentions. Although both roles are often carried out by one person, the distinction may be relevant in cases where the sender's intention is not expressed adequately in the text.

The intended target-text receiver is the addressee of the translation and is a decisive factor in the production of the TT. The definition of the target-text receiver should be part of the translation brief. Information about the target-text addressee (with regard to socio-cultural background, expectations, sensitivity or world knowledge) is of crucial importance for the translator. The addressee and the receiver differ in that the former is the prospective receiver seen from the text producer's standpoint while the latter is the person, group or institution that actually reads or listens to the text after it has been produced. The target-text user is the one who finally puts the TT to use, perhaps as training material, as a source of information or as a means of advertising.

It is important to note that the distinction of the agent roles is not absolute: two or more roles may be conflated in some cases and the functionalist approach confers very important position on the translator, the initiator and the target-text audience.

3. 2. 3   The Dethronement of the ST

The original text, or the ST is one of the most essential and important factors in each translation process. It is universally acknowledged that the ST must be carefully analyzed and profoundly understood for one thing and must be respected as authoritative for another. The traditional equivalence-based linguistic translation theory is source-text-centered. The source text is the first and foremost criterion to evaluate the translation. However, the role of the source text in functionalist approaches is radically different. It is adequately captured by Vermeer's idea of "dethronement" which indicates the source text is no longer the most authoritative and most important criterion for the translator's decisions; rather, it is a mere "offer of information", or the translator's "raw material" and just one of the various sources of information used by the translator. Faced with this "offer of information", the translator is entitled to choose the items he regards as interesting, useful or adequate to the desired purposes. Here two points must be made clear: (i) The term "dethronement" does not mean that the ST is unimportant in functionalist approach and one can translate without analyzing the ST carefully and adequately and working on it; (ii) From functionalist point of view, the translator, who is endowed with freedom and rights though, must be responsible and competent to make choices with reasoning.

3. 3 Translation Rules in Functionalist Approach

Functionalist theories, with the Skopos theory as its

core, contain two categories of rules: (i) the general rules which can be applied in any translation processes; (ii) the special rules that can only work in special cases. The Skopos rule and the loyalty rule are of the first group while the coherence rule and the fidelity rule belong to the second one. The following is a further elaboration of them.

The Skopos rule (also the aim rule): Skopostheory, first presented by Reiss and Vermeer in their book "General Foundations of Translation Theory", founded the cornerstone of the functionalist approach to translation. According to Skopostheory, the prime principle determining any translation process is the purposes of the overall translational action. It is the top-ranking rule for any translation. That is, the end justifies the means, or the translation purpose justifies the translation procedures.

The coherence rule (also the intra-textual coherence): The TT must be meaningful and acceptable to target culture receivers and sufficiently coherent with the receivers' situation. Obviously, this is similar to the idea of expressiveness in Yanfu's translation standard of "faithfulness, expressiveness and elegance".

The fidelity rule (also the inter-textual coherence): It means faithfulness of the TT to the ST, concerning the relationship between the ST and TT. It is similar to the idea of faithfulness or equivalence from traditional perspective.

The loyalty rule: The loyalty rule was put forward by Nord. She discovered two defects in radical functionalism: the first is the difficulty of translation caused by unique translation modes in different cultures and the second is caused by the relationship between the translator and the ST producer. In the former cases, the translator is responsible for explaining to the recipients the reason (for example in the preface) why he/she translates in that way; in the latter, the translator should respect the ST producer and coordinate the intended aim of the ST and TT. Accordingly, the loyalty refers to the responsibility the translators have toward their partners in translational interaction. It must not be mixed up with fidelity or faithfulness, concepts that usually refer to a relationship holding between the source and target texts. That's to say, loyalty is an interpersonal category referring to a social relationship between the translator and other participants.

The four rules are not of equal status within the framework of functionalist theories. The fidelity rule is subordinated to the coherence rule and both are subordinated to the Skopos rule, the top-ranking rule. The coherence rule and fidelity rule can not be applied to all cases. However, every translation process must comply with the Skopos rule and loyalty rule which are the backbones of functionalist theories. There are also some other rules in functionalist theories. The translator has the very right to choose the right rules in right situations. To sum up, the functionalist point of view on translation is: the skopos rule and the loyalty rule can substantially guide all translation processes while other rules are employed flexibly according to specific situations.

Equivalence or equivalent effect has long been regarded as the only criterion to evaluate translation. However, in functionalist framework, functional adequacy has become the criterion to assess translation. Adequacy refers to the qualities of a target text with regard to the translation brief. It is a dynamic concept related to the process of translational action and referring to the goal-oriented selection of signs. Equivalence, on the other hand, is a static, result-oriented concept describing a relationship between two texts or even on lower ranks, sentences, phrases or words and so on. In this sense, equivalence is only one of the various forms of adequacy from functionalist perspective.

Functionalist approach to translation paves a new way and makes significant contribution to translation studies. It marks a move away from static linguistic transfer and shifts the orientation to culture in translation studies. It views translation, not as a process of transcoding, but as an act of communication. It is oriented towards the function of the TT (prospective translation) rather than prescriptions of the ST (retrospective translation). It views the text as an integral part of the world and not as an isolated specimen of language (Snell-Hornby, 2001: 43). It initiates the poly-criterion of translation criticism, with greater theoretical magnanimity. It benefits much from culturology, act theory, communication theory, discourse analysis and reception theory and is therefore more scientific and feasible. (Wang Jingping & Yang Fan, 2021).

3.4   Enlightenment of the Theory on Advertising Translation

Considering the features of advertisement differing considerably from those of literature, this book maintains that the following points of enlightenment of functionalist theories fit well in with advertising translation, so as to justify the feasibility of the application of the theory to advertising translation.

①The extension of the concept of translation to translational action

Communication occurs both verbally and nonverbally. Experts in advertising state that nonverbal signs such as light, sound and motion play an increasingly important and even indispensable part in international advertising. Therefore, advertising translation covers all kinds of intercultural transfer, verbal and nonverbal. That is why Manttari prefers to speak of "message transmitters" which consist of textual material combined with other media such as picture, sounds and body movements. The concept of translational action in functionalist theories helps deal with the problems concerning nonverbal transfer while the traditional equivalence-based translation theories couldn't.

Besides, an advertiser sometimes depends on translators' professional opinions on the target culture to design or revise the advertisements. Such kind of translational action as a translator's professional advice is excluded out of the study of traditional translation. Functionalists, however, bring it into the domain of translation study and therefore further confirm the role and the status of translators in a world characterized by the division of labor.

②The insight in the idea of dethronement of the ST

The most conspicuous similarity between functionalist approach and advertisement lies in the target-audience-orientation. The ST is just one of the various sources of information used by the translator. The ST of an advertisement which targets at source language and cultural audience unavoidably includes some elements which are not suitable for the target language and cultural audience, so the translator is entitled to make use of any strategy which he/she thinks is appropriate to make his/her translation appealing to the target audience. In addition, some translations function as independent, autonomous, or self-sufficient texts in the target culture.

③The active participation of the translator in translating

From functionalist perspective, a competent translator is an expert with sound knowledge of bilingual, bicultural and advertising as well as a visible creative producer of the TT, thus playing a crucial and initiative role in the translation process. This happens to accord with the role of the advertising-maker who should be equipped with adequate knowledge of every aspects of target audience and target culture.

④The emphasis on the role of target receiver

In functional theory, the target receiver is assigned a higher status and a more influential role, which is consistent with one of the most important rules in advertising: emphasis on the role of target audience, including their world knowledge, expectation, consuming customs, the social values they cling to. The emphasis on the target audience also answers the question as to whom the translator should serve: the ST producer or the target receiver.

⑤The provision of theoretical basis for some unconventional translation methods

The functional translation theory provides a theoretical basis for some unconventional translation strategies and methods such as adaptation, rewriting, addition and abridgement which are excluded from the domain of translation by traditional equivalence-based translation theories but frequently employed and prove to be effective in advertising translation practice.

⑥Vocative text and functional translation

Advertising is a type of practical writing as well as a typical vocative text type. The most conspicuous point it shares with functionalist theories is that they attach great importance to the expected communicative function of the TT and the expectancy of the target addressees, so vocative text such as advertising deserves functional translation.

Chapter 4   Strategies and Methods of Advertising Translation in Light of Functionalist Approach

On the basis of the previous exploration of advertising and functionalist approach, this chapter, with four sections, is intended to go further to probe into the specific issues of translating advertisements, from general guiding principles to specific translation techniques with many authentic examples. Before elaboration, it is necessary to distinguish two important terminologies in this chapter: strategy and method. According to "Oxford Advanced Learner's Dictionary of Current English", the term "strategy" refers to skillfully planning generally, or general direction and planning as "method" indicates a planned way of doing something. Simply speaking, "strategy" is used to describe a higher-level decision and general direction of an action while "method" is taken to describe the specific way of doing something. In the translation studies, translation strategies, as Jaaskelainen stated, "are a set of (loosely formulated) rules or principles which a translator uses to reach the goals determined by the translating situation in the most effective way" (Chesterman, 1997: 88).

4.1 Strategy vs. Method: Target-language-culture Orientation or Source-language-culture Orientation

Generally speaking, the two basic strategies in translating have been target-language-culture orientation and source-language-culture orientation. Early in 1813, Schleiermacher in his work "Ueber die verschiedenen Methoden des Uebersezens (On the Different Methods of Translating)" argued that "the translator can either leave the author in peace as much as possible and moves the reader towards him, or he can leave the reader in peace as much as possible and moves the author towards him" (Snell-Hornby, 2001: 10). Here, Schleiermacher maintained the two basic strategies in translation. The former is "source-language culture oriented strategy", also called "alienation" or "foreignization", in which the translator tries to retain the images and features of the source language and culture so as to keep the "foreignness" of the ST; the latter is "target-language-culture oriented strategy", also called "domest-ication" or "adaptation", in which the translator strives to substitute or interpret the images and features of source language and culture with corresponding images and features familiar in the target language and culture in order to cater to the target audience's taste.

Whether to adopt target-language-culture oriented strategy or to take source-language-culture oriented strategy in translation has been a disputable issue for a long time. In contemporary Western schools of translation, Eugene A. Nida, who put forward the concept of "dynamic" or "functional equivalence" in translation, can be regarded as a representative of the advocators of target-language-culture orientation. The representative of source-language-culture orientation is no doubt Lawrence Venuti who, from the perspective of deconstructionism, put forward "resistance translation strategy" which avoids fluency but highlights foreignness of translated text in target culture. Similar dispute over literal translation (i.e. source-language-culture orientation) and free translation (i.e. target-language-culture orientation) have been existing for more than 70 years. Zhao Jingsheng (赵景升) is one of the representatives of those who favor the target-language-culture orientation while Lu Xun (鲁迅) is the representative of those who prefer to the source-language-culture orientation. The controversy over these two translation strategies continues today and seems without end, just as Han Wei (2021: 248) have claimed that there exists translation, and the debates on them are sure to be endless.

As two basic translation strategies, source-language-culture orientation and target-language-culture orientation bear their own advantages and disadvantages respectively. The source-language-culture oriented strategy, recognizing the objective existence of cultural differences, going with the general trend of cultural communication and ferment, exerts a positive influence on intercultural communication in a long run, but whether the target text can be accepted widely or not relies, to a great extent, on the test of time and practice and the acceptability varies from stage to stage. The target-language-culture orientation can avoid this problem and give full play to the advantages of target language, thus enhancing the readability of TT. It, however, sticking to respective linguistic convention and indifferent to the historical tide of cultural ferment, takes a negative attitude towards cultural differences and consequently does little good for intercultural communication and globalization. Accordingly, the two strategies, complementary and interdependent, couldn't be judged and evaluated with the dichotomies of right/wrong, or good/bad, just as Guo Jianzhong (1998) states that both are valuable considering the author's intention, text type, translation purpose and readers' requirements.

As stated before, while "strategy" is used to describe a higher-level decision and general direction of an action, "method" is taken to describe the specific way of doing something. The translation methods more often seen in practice are transliteration, literal translation, free translation, adaptation, imitation and rewriting. Transliteration, according to Catford, refers to a process in which SL graphological units are replaced by TL graphological units (Mark & Moira, 2004: 189). For example, the conversion of "coffee" to " 咖啡 " and "Olympus" to " 奥林巴斯 " is typical transliteration. As for literal translation, Catford offers a definition based on the notion of the unit of translation: he argues that literal translation takes word-for-word translation as its starting point, although because of the necessity of conforming to TL grammar, the final TT may also display group-group or clause-clause equivalence (ibid.: 95). Free translation means a type of translation in which more attention is paid to produce a naturally reading TT than to preserving the ST wording intact. Also known as sense-for-sense translation, it contrasts sharply with literal and word-for-word translation (ibid.: 62). Free translations are thus generally more "TL-oriented" than literal translation. Adaptation usually implies that considerable changes have been made in order to make the text more suitable for a specific audience (e.g. children) or for the particular purpose behind the translation (ibid: 3).

It is considered "the freest form of translation" by Peter Newmark (2002: 46). Addition and abridgement are included in this category. Rewriting, a term introduced by Lefevere, indicates a range of processes, including translation, which can be said to reinterpret, alter or manipulate an original text in some way. It is closely connected with the political and literary power structures which operate within a given culture, as the processes of adaptation and manipulation which rewriters perform generally lead to the production of texts which reflect the dominant ideology and poetics (Mark & Moira, 2004: 147). Among the translation methods mentioned above, some are more frequently adopted in the source-language-culture orientation such as transliteration and literal translation while others, such as free translation, adaptation and rewriting are taken more often in the translation with target-language-culture orientation. Of course, the corresponding relationship of translation methods and strategies is not fixed and absolute but dynamic and relative. Furthermore, all the methods have their own shining points as well as limitations. For a given text, what methods should be employed is decided by such contextual variables as text type, translation purpose, target readership, translators' personal style, etc. Incidentally, traditional equivalence-based linguistic translation theories hold that adaptation and rewriting are not translation at all.

4. 2   A Test of the Strategies and the Methods in Advertising Translation: A Questionnaire

4. 2. 1   Theoretical Foundation for Designing the Questionnaire

As a break with the traditional translation ideas and an important complement to translation theories, functionalist approach to translation, raised by K. Reiss, H. J. Vermeer, J. H. Manttari and C. Nord, has opened up a new perspective to translation studies. It, having deconstructed the definition of translation itself, dethroned the sovereign position of ST and solved the eternal dilemmas of free vs. literal translation, adaptation vs. alienation, good interpreters vs. slavish translators and so on, confirms the foremost and focal role of the translation purpose and the intended function of TT in target culture in the option of translation strategy and methods. That is, "the end justifies the means". The three possible kinds of purpose in the field of translation can be distinguished as: (i) the general purpose of the translator in the translation process; (ii) the communicative purpose aimed at by the target text in the target situation; (iii) the purpose of a particular translation strategy or procedure.

Nevertheless, the term "skopos" usually refers to the purpose of the TT. Indeed, the purpose of the translator in advertising translation is subordinate to the ultimate purpose of advertisements: to promote sales of various products or to popularize the use of services, so the task of translators in advertising translation is to help the advertiser to build up the image of a product or that of an enterprise and promote sales in the target market. Whether the translation of an advertisement is good or not will make a great impact on the success or failure of the campaign in exploring a new market.

As discussed in Chapter 2, the overriding function of advertising is to persuade or manipulate the potential consumers to buy a product and accept the ideas, values and lifestyle that are associated with the product. In order to achieve this function, a translated advertising text must be easily comprehensible and widely acceptable to the target audience. Therefore, the task of the advertiser as well as the translator is to make sure that the advertisement is attractive and easy to understand at first sight either in content or in form. That's to say, the translation of advertisements must adapt to target language style and target cultural concept so as to exploit the persuasion at its best. If the advertisement seems strange and baffling, the target audience will lose interest in reading on and pay no attention to what is advertised and of course no action of purchase will take place.

So far, it is clear that both content and form of the source advertising text are subordinated to the persuasive function that the target advertisement is designed to achieve. As a result, only when the original advertisement is adapted to the target language and cultural standards when it is translated, can the target audience easily understand what is advertised and be likely to accept the persuasion and buy the advertised product. As Nord claims, "Different communicative functions may require different translation strategies. If the purpose of the translation is to keep function of the text invariant, function markers often have to be adapted to target-culture standards" (Nord, 2001: 45).

Based on this foundation, a small-scaled questionnaire on the response of the target audiences to the different versions of translated advertising texts is conducted so as to find out the very strategy and method that can help achieve the special purpose of advertising and develop the special persuasive function at its best.

4. 2. 2   An Introduction to the Questionnaire

The purpose: To find out the very strategy and method that can help achieve the intended function of translated advertising text in target culture at its best.

The content: Two advertisements and different versions of translated texts are provided with corresponding questions to be answered (seen in the Appendix B).

The respondents:

Group 1: 50 English-speaking foreigners from all walks of life and of all ages from 23 to 60.

Group 2: 50 Chinese undergraduates and postgraduates majoring in English language and literature.

The method: Analyzing the responses objectively by calculation of the probability to arrive at reasonable conclusions.

4.2.3 The Analysis of the Result of the Questionnaire

As can be seen from Figure 4.1, 35 of 50 Chinese students think Version B translation of Ad. No.1 is the best while only 2 of 50 English-speakers favor it. Version C is regarded as the best advertising slogan by English-speakers as only 9 Chinese students think it a good translation. That's to say, 70% Chinese label Version B as the best while 88% foreigners prefer Version C. The quality of the translations should be judged by the answers from Group 1 since they are target audience rather than Group 2 who serves the target audience of the original Chinese advertisement. Therefore, Version C is the best and Version B, the worst to serve as an advertising slogan in target market.

Figure 4.1   The Result of the Questionnaire

Ad.	Question	Respondents	Answers		
			A	B	C
No.1	1	Group 1 (English-speakers)	4	2	44
		Group 2 (Chinese students)	6	35	9
No. 2	2	Group 1 (English-speakers)	0	47	3
	3	Group 1 (English-speakers)	4	43	3
	4	Group 1 (English-speakers)	0	44	6

Obviously, the three translations have all made some degree of adaptation. In Version A, two subordinate clauses, "品质优良" "书写滑润" and one adjective phrase "美观大方" are converted into three noun phrases "First-class quality" "smooth writing" and "elegant design", to conform to the rule of brevity and conciseness of English advertising language. In Version B, the translator makes greater but inappropriate adaptation as a result of negative transfer of culture. Antithetical couplet as a typical Chinese folk culture is quite popular among Chinese since aesthetically Chinese people are delighted with symmetry, so such kind of writing skill is commonly employed in advertising. Seeing through culturally tinted glasses, the translator takes it for granted that antithetical couplet would do as well in English advertising as it does in Chinese advertising. And the translator is not alone in this point since 35 students, some of whom are potential professional translators or translation researchers, stand with her. Therefore, the translator makes adjustment of the ST with a good intention to improve the translation which turns out to be poor in effect in that it, however adapted in language, adheres to the aesthetic preference of the source culture rather than that of the target culture. Then what leads to the popularity of Version C among the target audience? Adaptation is also made in Version C. Firstly, the rhetoric device of alliteration is created in it which bestows on the advertisement the sense of ease and humor, which impresses the target audience and makes the translation successful. Secondly, the brand name is literally rendered as "China" not transliterated as "Zhonghua" which serves no more than a pile of letters for English-speakers who do not know Chinese. In addition, the whole slogan, with concise language and lively rhythm, reads smoothly and meets the satisfaction of the target audience to the greatest extent. On the whole, Version A and Version B tend to be source-language-culture oriented though some degree of adaptation is made while Version C employs the target-language-culture oriented strategy with appropriate and ingenious adaptation.

As is shown in Figure 4.1, 47 among 50 (i.e. 94%) English-speakers maintain that Version B of Ad. No. 2 offers the more important and useful information, 86% of them hold that the language of Version B is more acceptable in their culture and 88% tend to take action when reading Version B in comparison with none for Version A.

Obviously, the original Chinese text functions as an acceptable, frequently-seen and successful advertisement in Chinese's eyes. Version A, equivalent to the ST semantically, syntactically and stylistically, remains a perfect translation from the traditional equivalence-based linguistic approaches. Whereas it encounters great failure among the target audience in that very few of them regard it as a useful, readable and impressive advertisement as is clear in Figure 4.1. The real problem with Version A lies in that the translator, only bearing in mind the ST and the standard of equivalence in meaning, neglects the important role of target cultural elements and thus the intended function of the TT. Firstly, the first sentence "Pudong Shanghai is the 14th hotel opened by Shangri-La Hotel Management Group in China." gives no information the consumers are interested in but more like an introduction of the rapid development of Shangri-La Hotel in China. Secondly, the measuring unit of area "square meter" is incomprehensible for common English-speakers just as the "square foot" does for ordinary Chinese people. Thirdly, the introduction to the categorization of the guest rooms is totally unnecessary, for the Hotel Industry has been long developed in western countries and consumers are fairly familiar with the specification of it in various kinds of hotels. Lastly, the detailed introduction to the cuisine does nothing but imposes unnecessary burden of compression on the target audiences who do not anticipate difficulties or obscurities in advertising.

By contrast, Version B, though not equivalent to the ST, is thought of as useful in information, natural in language and convincing in effect by the overwhelming majority of the target audiences investigated. Bearing in mind the target cultural elements and the intended function of the TT, the translator makes adaptation to great extent by addition of information of the location and the convenient transportation of the hotel which are more than welcome by businessmen and the breathtaking views which surely attract both businessmen and sightseers, and replacement of the redundant and obscure introduction to the guestrooms and food services by brief, general and impressive description.

The above analysis briefly explains that a translator of advertising translation should be well-equipped with not only bilingual but also bicultural knowledge as well. And advertising translation should take the target-language-culture oriented strategy with flexible employment of various methods to accord with the intended function of the target advertising texts in the target culture. The translator thus should make great efforts to get rid of the influence of mother tongue and try to think in the target audience's shoes.

4.3   Analysis of Real-life Advertising Translation

Advertising translation is involved when advertisements created in one culture have to be translated for use in another culture. Advertising translation does not merely imply finding linguistic equivalents in the TL since advertisements are no doubt reflection of society and culture. Then how does real-life advertising translation operate? The very question is to be answered in the following presentation and exploitation of some authentic examples, either successful or a failure in the target markets.

First of all, the translation of brands is to be investigated on the basis of Figure 4.2. As is clear in Figure 4.2, examples in Group 4 and Group 5, which have proved fairly successful in target market, are rewritings rather than translation, let alone good or bad, if judged from traditional equivalence-based perspective of translation which confines translation to faithful reproduction of the ST or the replacement of the material in one language by equivalent material in another.

Figure 4.2   Translation of Brand Names (1)

		ST	TT	Translation Methods
Group 1	Kodak	柯达	transliteration
	Parker	派克	
Group 2	General	通用	literal translation
	Playboy	花花公子	
Group 3	Bausch&Lomb	博士伦	transliteration and meaning implication
	Johnson's	强生	
Group 4	Seven-up	七喜	literal translation and adaptation
	Goldlion	金利来	
Group 5	Sprite	雪碧	creation
	Rejoice	飘柔	

Secondly, the translation of advertising slogans is going to be discussed. Undoubtedly, all translations in Figure 4.3 are quite successful in persuading the target audience to take action. Examples in Group 1 employ word-for-word translation skill in that the ST and TT are equivalent semantically, syntactically and stylistically. But in Group 2, the translations are unfaithful either in meaning or in form to the original texts. The literal translation of "For next generation" is "为了下一代" while additional meaning occurs in translated text "新一代的选择". "The relentless pursuit of perfection", a noun phrase, is adapted to two four-character phrases which commonly appear in Chinese advertisements since Chinese people prefer symmetry aesthetically. Therefore, in these two examples, what the translators manage to do is to transfer the original ideas or thoughts expressed in the ST to TT with the preference of target language and culture taken into consideration instead of a direct transfer. In Group 3, however, it is very difficult to find resemblance between the source texts and targettexts. Literal translation of "Connecting people" （将人们联系起来）is obviously faraway from what "科技以人为本" conveys. Similarly, the back translation of "科技以人为本" has nothing to do with the ST as well. The same problem lies in the second example in this group. Apparently, the source texts in these two examples serve nothing but offer of some material which remains one of the various sources of information provided for the translator who finally gives up the ideas conveyed by the source texts and creates two new advertising slogans in the way the target language and culture prefer.

Figure 4.3　Translation of Advertising Slogans

	ST	TT	Translation Methods
Group 1	Let's make things better. (Phillips)	让我们做得更好！	word-for-word translation
	Challenge the limits. (Samsung)	挑战极限！	

(to be continued)

	ST	TT	Translation Methods
Group 2	For next generation. (Pepsi-cola)	新一代的选择。	adaptation
	The relentless pursuit of perfection. (Lexus-automobile)	专注完美，近乎苛求。	
Group 3	Connecting people. (Nokia)	科技以人为本。	creation
	It's all within your reach. (AT&T)	联络世界，触及未来。	

So far, the analysis of the above examples demonstrates that real-life advertising translation is not a passive activity of reproducing faithfully the message of the ST or seeking the equivalent between ST and TT as required by the traditional equivalence-based linguistic approaches but a dynamic activity of creative interpretation in which adaptations or adjustments of the source text to the target language and culture are usually intentionally made by translators to achieve the intended function of advertising in the target culture. Obviously, the traditional concepts and theories fail to encompass and account for the unconventional translation strategies and methods such as adaptation and rewriting. However, as Toury states, "If a theory fails to explain each phenomenon in the activity of translation, it is the theory that is faulty and need correction but not the phenomenon" (Zhao Yingying, 2019). The very theory which can overcome the defects of traditional theories is functionalist approach to translation which provides theoretical basis for the unconventional translation strategies. In a word, real-life advertising translation is not trapped in the confinement of the source language and culture and the suffering of seeking equivalence but remains an active, multidimensional, dynamic, creative and target-language-culture oriented activity with the ST only one of the various sources of information for reference. Accordingly, the target-language-culture-oriented strategy and flexible use of various methods are widely adopted, consciously or unconsciously, by a great number of competent translators in practice, which is in tune with the conclusion of the questionnaire.

As stated by functionalist school, translating is a complex and purposeful human activity involving many choices and processes. Accordingly, the option of translation strategies and methods is determined by many contextual variables a competent translator should keep in mind rather than the subjective decision of the translator alone. In light of functionalist theory, the purpose of the overall translational action or the intended function of the TT in target situation should be the first concern and decisive factor in the whole translation process including selecting translation strategy and methods. As detailed in Chapter 2, advertising, as a very practical type of writing, differs greatly from literature whose ultimate purpose is cultural exchange. However, the ultimate purpose of advertising is to promote sales or popularize the use of services and the overwhelming function of advertising remains persuasion and manipulation of the potential consumers to buy a product or accept the ideas, values and lifestyles associated with the product. Therefore, on the basis of the questionnaire and the analysis of real-life phenomena in advertising translation, with the specialty of advertising taken into account, the present study, under the guidance of German functionalist theory, proposes tentatively that advertising translation should employ the target-language-culture oriented strategy with flexible utilization of various translation methods, especially adaptation and rewriting which are excluded from the domain of translation study by traditional equivalence-based translation theories so as to achieve the special purpose and function of advertising at its best.

4.4   Application of the Functionalist Strategy and Methods in Advertising Translation

As mentioned in Chapter 2, a complete written adver-tisement is usually made up of five component parts: headline, body text, slogan, brand name and illustration, among which brand name and slogan play a special role in advertisements, so the following sections will discuss the application of target-language-culture oriented strategy and methods in translating brand name, slogan and advertising text.

4. 4. 1   The Translation of Brand Names

Brand name, an identifying symbol of a product, generally gives first impression to the consumers and thus plays an important part in influencing their decisions. Hence, when exploring a new market in another country, it is very important, even decisive to a great extent to see that the translation of a brand name satisfies target audience's taste. In other words, the translation of brand name must be target-language-culture oriented with flexible use of various translation methods. In any culture, a brand name should have the following features: (i) accorded with the characteristics of the products; (ii) containing a sense of symbolism to start delightful imagination in people's minds; (iii) being easily remembered and pronounced (Jing Yanjun, 2021: 81).

In the translation of brand names, exact transliteration or literal translation is desired as long as it can meet the three requirements for a brand name and thus capture the new market as widely as possible, for example, Ford—福特; Olympus—奥林巴斯; Crown—皇冠; Panda—熊猫; 联想—Legend; 海尔—Haier; 鸭鸭—Ya Ya. It goes without saying that this is an ideal condition in translation. Under such circumstances, any adaptation or adjustment is both unnecessary and unbearable. But in most cases, absolute transliteration or literal translation leads to big failures in opening up the target market owing to the great differences of language and culture of the ST and the TT, as can be seen in Figure 4.4 "轻身减肥片", originally translated as "Obesity-reducing Tablets", was expected to sell well in America where keeping-fit is in fashion, but unfortunately no one was interested in it. Market investigation finds that the problem lies in the translation of the brand name which violates consumer's psychology because "obese" in English means "extremely fat or unhealthily fat" so that no consumer is willing to call himself an obese man. Later, the revised translation, "Slimming Pills", adapted to cater to target consumers' pleasure, proves to be quite successful in broadening the market. "杜康", the brand name for a spirit, if faithful to the ST, can be transliterated as Dukang which is nothing but a combination of six letters in the eyes of Westerners. However, the translation, "Bacchus" by means of rewriting brings people associations of good spirits because Bacchus is the God for Spirits in Ancient Greek mythology. "彩虹", the trademark for a TV set, is translated to "Irico" instead of rainbow. In Western cultures, rainbow connotes momentary beauty, apt to arouse distrust in the quality of the product. What's more, it is much less rich in associative meaning than Irico blended by Irix and Corporation. Irix is the God for Rainbow in Greek mythology who is responsible for delivering good things. Hence, Irico, with pleasant sounds and fine artistic mood, proves to be quite adequate and successful in promoting sales. "喜鹊" bed sheet may encounter great trouble in promoting sales in international market if the brand name is literally rendered as "Magpie", for it is related to gossipy persons in English cultures which is quite different from the good connotation of "lucky bird that heralds good news" in Chinese. As a result, the brand name is adapted ingeniously into "Luckybird" in English.

Figure 4.4　Translation of Brand Names (2)

	ST	TT1	TT2
1	轻身减肥片	Obesity-reducing Tablets	Slimming Pills
2	杜康（酒）	Dukang	Bacchus
3	彩虹（电器）	Rainbow	Irico
4	喜鹊（床单）	Magpie	Luckybird
5	昂立一号（药品）	Ang Li One	Only One
6	Coca-cola	肯蜡蝌蚪	可口可乐
7	Mercedes-Benz	默塞得斯·本茨	奔驰
8	Poison	毒药	百爱神
9	KENT	接吻不用教／肯特	健牌
10	Puma	美洲狮	彪马

"昂立一号" (medicine) is rendered not as "Ang Li One" because "Ang Li" bears no meaning at all in English but as "Only One" which shows the peculiar quality and effect of the medicine, thus meeting consumers' psychological demands in individualism-oriented cultures. Coca-cola, a soft drink, once translated into "肯蜡蝌蚪" which, awkward to read and the worst, apt to cause queasy feeling, encountered big failure in Chinese market, became a widely-known and favored drink when changed the translation into "可口可乐" which reads smoothly and conveys such information about the product and consumers' response after tasting as "可口" (good taste) and "乐" (happy or pleasant). "默塞得斯·本茨", the exact transliteration of the automobile, "Mercedes-Benz", is hard to pronounce and remember for Chinese and no more than a pile of characters while "奔驰" not only reads smoothly but also creates a vivid scene of an automobile flying in the road. Poison, the brand name of a perfume, taking advantage of opposite thinking, won great favor of female westerners who pursue the wild and vulgar exotic flavor. However, since the female Chinese tend to be comparatively conservative, introverted, reserved and gentle, the brand name is rendered as "百爱神" meaning the God which brings you abundant love and it is sold very well in China for many years. But in recent years with the intensification of international exchange, more and more young female Chinese are increasingly open and trying to highlight individuality and specialty, so " 毒药香水 " has been employed and gained more and more market share. This case reveals fully that the target audience remains dynamic so that a competent translator should know clearly the dynamic factors so as to adjust the translation to cater to their taste. KENT, the brand name of cigarettes, is the abbreviation of the English slang "kiss ever never teaches". Since the Chinese do not have the same cultural experience as those in English-speaking countries to fully appreciate the humor and capture the implied information about the irresistible power of the product, it would not make much sense to translate it into " 接吻不用教 " by using the foreignizing strategy. The transliteration " 肯特 " bears no information but a slight foreign taste. Whereas, the creation " 健 " which in Chinese is very concise but contains rich meanings such as " 健康 " (healthy), " 健壮 " (strong), " 健美 " (graceful), describes the irresistible advantage of the cigarettes from different angles and is easy for Chinese consumers to associate with the brand name and to remember. No wonder the brand of cigarettes remains so famous in China nowadays. Puma, the brand name of sports shoes, tends to imply that the one wearing it would walk or run fast and look powerful like a puma which, in English, means a large brown American animal of the cat family, also called a cougar and mountain lion, with the Chinese equivalent of " 美洲狮 ". However, the common Chinese people have little idea about " 美洲狮 " and it seems a bit ferocious and thus couldn't win the favor. But the domesticated translation " 彪马 " which, similar to "puma" in pronunciation, expresses the meaning of "a hefty horse", displays for consumers a compelling image of a strong horse running swiftly as wind, managing to imply the good quality of the sports shoes as horse in Chinese is closely associated with such qualities as "friendly, strong, well-proportioned and swift" and " 彪 " has another homophone " 飚 " which indicates as swift as wind.

But unfortunately, due to poor knowledge of target language and culture, some Chinese enterprises fail to promote sales of their products in international markets. For instance, " 芳芳爽身粉 ", with the translation of "Fang Fang Talcum Powder", is unsalable in the western market because "Fang Fang" means "poisonous teeth" in English. Li Guisheng (1996) suggests that it be rendered as "Fragrance" (芳香) or "Fun Fun" (开心) which the author of this book thinks good and feasible. " 飞鸽 ", a well-known brand of bicycle, is unfortunately translated into "Flying Pigeon" which puzzled the Westerners in that there are two words equivalent to Chinese " 鸽子 ": pigeon and dove, the former being the bird shot for food by hunters while the latter being the one symbolizing peace. As for it, Li Guisheng provides two suggested translations: one is Flying Dove and the other is Flying Eagle, for eagle is strong and powerful and there is a very famous brand of bicycle called Eagle in England. " 紫罗兰 ", a popular brand for men's underwear in China, was cold-shouldered in foreign market in that the transla-tion "Pansy" connotes derogatory meaning in English— an effeminate young man or male homosexual. The author of this book suggests "Violet" as its translation. " 金鸡 ", an alarm clock made in China, is quite popular and widely known in Chinese market because " 金 " is a sign of valuable and precious and " 雄鸡 " (cock) is usually good and positive in associations, such as " 雄鸡报晓 " （Cocks herald the break of a day） and " 闻鸡起舞 " (to perform a sword-dance as soon as cocks begin to crow). However, few Western consumers are interested in it while seeing "Golden Cock" because "cock" is often related to male sex organ in Western cultures. The author suggests "Golden Rooster" tentatively. Guangzhou " 五羊 " bicycle, which symbolizes good fortune as one wishes in Chinese culture has to face sales problem in the West because of the literal translation of brand name "Five Rams" which is associated with recklessness and dangerousness in the western culture. It is also inappropriate to translate it into "Five Goats" because goat is often used derogatorily or humorously referring to a man who is very active sexually. The author suggests creation of a new brand, such as "Seven Dogs" especially for Western market, for both the figure "seven" and the animal "dog" associate with such meanings as lucky, lively and friendly in Western cultures.

4. 4. 2 The Translation of Advertising Slogans

Slogan originally means "battle cry". In advertising, a slogan is mainly aimed at maintaining the continuity of an advertising campaign and holding consumers' interest and promoting sales of the product. Normally an advertising slogan consists of just a few words, which are smooth to read and easy to remember. That's to say, an ideal slogan should be simple, clear, attractive, memorable and persuasive. Therefore, when translating slogans, a wise translator should take into full consideration of the features of target language and culture and think in the target audience's shoes.

In the first place, on linguistic level, translation of advertising slogans means, rather than a merely mechanical transfer of linguistic signs, a complex process in which the translator should take full advantage of target language after probing into the target advertising language to cater for target audience's taste. The following presents a deep and detailed comparative study of translating advertising slogans.

(2) ST: Taste that beats the other cold. (Pepsi-cola ad.)
TT: 百事可乐，冷饮之王。（严琦，2021: 71）
(3) ST: A diamond is forever. (De Beers ad.)
TT: 钻石恒久远，一颗永流传。（贾文波，2018: 130）
(4) ST: Intel Inside. (Intel ad.)

TT: 一颗奔腾的心。

(5) ST:（燕窝）滋补养颜，常服能保青春。

TT1: Regular consumption of Bird's Nest keeps one's skin and face youthful.

TT2: Regular taking of Bird's Nest keeps you looking youthful. （贾文波，2018: 130）

(6) ST: 喝一杯即饮柠檬茶令你怡神醒脑！

TT1: Drinking a glass of Instant Lemon Tea makes you refreshed.

TT2: For Refreshment? A Glass of Instant Lemon Tea!

（张旖璇，刘艳，2021: 23）

(7) ST: 弘扬体育精神，促进国际往来。

TT1: Spreading over the physical spirits and promoting international communications.

TT2: Promote sportsmanship and international exchanges. (ibid.: 24)

Four-character compounds and parallelism are two typical linguistic features in Chinese language. Four-character compounds usually convey profound meanings in very concise structures with strong rhythm as is clearly reflected in Example (2) while parallelism is used for emphasis and heightening the effectiveness of expressions by balancing word with word, phrase with phrase and sentence with sentence such as Example (3). These two linguistic devices are widely employed in Chinese advertisements due to their expressiveness and effectiveness. With the help of these devices, the translation of slogans seems to be smooth to read, easy to remember and impress deeply. As for Example (4), alliteration is employed in the ST, with which the original text not only illustrates the important position of CPU, but also strengthens the consumer's impression of the brand name "Intel". But the literal translation "内装英特尔（中央处理器）" may be, however, hard to arouse any attention in Chinese consumers, let alone take action. However, with adoption of targetlanguage oriented strategy, the translated text "一颗奔腾的心" contains a metaphor and pun in that "一颗心" (a heart) is used to metaphorize the important position of CPU, while "奔腾" means doubly: the major product of Intel Co. Ltd, "Pentium" and the speedy calculating capability of Intel's product. The TT1 in Example (5) obviously does not accord with the feature of advertising English which prefers generalization, colloquialism and popularization. "Consumption", a formal word, rarely appears in daily situations among common people compared with "taking". "One's skin and face" seems too literary. Hence, the second translation is no doubt better considering the special functions of advertising slogans. In Example (6), the TT1, faithful to the original form and content, is dull and insipid, though. TT2, putting an interrogative sentence at the beginning to arouse consumers' curiosity and then employing an imperative sentence to achieve a persuasive effect, creates successfully a quick, jumping and lively rhythm, to prompt consumers to buy in a kind and friendly way. In Example (7), TT1, a typical word-for-word translation, neglects the linguistic conventions of target audiences who expect to see a brief and inspiring slogan instead of a long and redundant one and is therefore, by no means satisfying. In comparison, TT2, by combining two verbs in ST into one "promote" and employing more natural and accurate expressions to stand for two noun phrases, accords with the taste and cognitive process of English-speaking readers and is acceptable and efficient accordingly.

In the second place, as a form of intercultural comm-unication, advertising translation involves cultural transfer as well. The advertisement that is quite successful in one culture may not necessarily mean the same in another because of cultural obstacles. Therefore, the mechanical rendering into the target language with ignorance of cultural differences will undoubtedly fail to arouse target consumers' interest and desire to buy the commodities, especially the advertising translation between English and Chinese which belong to different language families and culture systems. For example:

(8) ST: He just killed the last dragon!
TT: 柯达胶卷，属于你的家庭快乐。
(9) ST: 让 WIC 妇孺计划帮助你。

TT: Let WIC work for you.

(10) ST: 红玫相机新奉献。（Red Rose ad.）

TT: My love is like a Red Rose. （严琦，2021: 70）

The first example above is an advertisement for Kodak, an American-made film. The advertising slogan in America is that "He just killed the last dragon" accompanied with a corresponding scene in which a little boy is trampling on a dragon with a bloody sword in his hand. It is undoubtedly in line with Western people's worldview and value orientation in that in Western cultures, "dragon" is the symbol of an evil and fierce monster and the conquest of the last dragon symbolizes a victory of venture and courage. Obviously, this advertising is successful in arousing an empathetic chord of western consumers and luring them into buying the product. However, to Chinese people, " 龙 ", sacred and auspicious, symbolizes the ancestor of Chinese nation, so no Chinese consumers would appreciate and accept the advertisement in which a little Western boy is trampling on a dragon with the caption "He just killed the last dragon". Moreover, Chinese Advertising Act regulates that any advertising related to terror and violence is forbidden. In order to explore Chinese market, Kodak company adopts the strategy of target-culture orientation and the method of rewriting, presenting the advertisement " 柯达胶卷，属于你的家庭快乐 ". Though radically different from the original one, the

Chinese version can strike Chinese consumers' hearts and attract their interest because Chinese value orientations attach much importance to family and home. In accordance with functionalist approach, the prime principle determining any translation process is the Skopos of the overall translational action, which covers all forms of intercultural transfer, including those that do not involve any source or target texts(Nord, 2001: 13). For the sake of promoting sales, Kodak presents the magnificent feat to American consumers and the family happiness to Chinese consumers. In Example (9), the phrase " 帮助 " in the ST is rendered into "work for" in the TT, for in China people think highly of the help among people while in the West, people highlight the individual spirits and have high sense of responsibility to their work. The adaptation makes the meaning of the TT more tangible and concrete, that is, by working for you, we help you out of your trouble. In Example (10), the English version imitated the famous love poem, "My love is like a red, red rose." written by Robert Burns, the well-known Scotland poet. As a result, the slogan helps to catch the consumers' attention quickly and impresses them deeply. Clearly, it is a good example with the general knowledge of target audience taken into consideration.

To sum up, as advertising is intended to build up a good image of the advertised product and to promote sales at last, advertising slogans are specially designed to be attractive, persuasive, and unforgettable to provide continuity for an advertising campaign. In order to render the original slogans as attractive, distinctive and effective as possible, translators should take advantages of the linguistic characteristics in the target cultural context. Hence, target-language-culture oriented strategy in translation is necessary and inevitable.

4. 4. 3   The Translation of Advertising Text

The definition of text tends to be very broad in common textual analysis. In this book, the text refers broadly to the linguistic units larger than sentence. In accordance with functionalist approach to translation, intertextual coherence (fidelity) is subordinated to intratextual coherence and both of them are subordinated to the Skopos rule. Hence, while translating advertisements, the translator should try every possible means such as addition, abridgement and rewriting to ensure the coherence of TT itself and the fulfillment of its function of persuasion at its best. For example:

(11) ST: 团结湖北京烤鸭店为全聚德挂炉烤鸭。为保证宾客品尝精美风味，全部现吃现烤。精选纯北京白鸭，以果木挂炉烤制，只需四十分钟就能品尝到为您特别烤制的色泽枣红，香酥脆嫩，浓香四溢的正宗烤鸭。

TT: Tuanjiehu Beijing Roast Duck Restaurant uses only the finest Beijing Ducks which are only roasted after you place your order. Preparation takes 40 minutes after which we will server you with a delicious, golden red Beijing Duck with crunchy skin.（肖新英，2021: 40）

Tuanjiehu（团结湖）is a branch of the famous roast duck restaurant, Quanjude（全聚德）. The aim of this piece of advertisement is to advertise for the branch restaurant instead of the main one. The ST emphasizes the good quality of their food and services by laying stress on the promptness of services, high-quality raw materials and special cooking instruments. The original text puts the restaurant name "全聚德" at conspicuous position, which has been famous in history and still attractive nowadays. The name has been widely known and loved by the Chinese people. Undoubtedly, it can function as an attractive point and highlight the position of the branch restaurant in the original text. However, most native English speakers are not familiar with this food brand. If the English readers read a sentence like "after the recipe of the Quanjude, a famous roast duck restaurant in Beijing", they will most probably remember "Quanjude" and neglect "Tuanjiehu", which is not in accordance with the original intention to advertise for "Tuanjiehu". Meanwhile, such phrases as "挂炉烤鸭" and "以果木挂炉烤制", which are used in the SL to show the food culture, are deleted for the demand function. Even most Chinese can not understand the cooking instruments thoroughly, let alone English readers grown up in a completely different culture. Such phrases can hardly make sense to the English-speaking audience, so are deleted to meet the translation skopos. After the adaptation, the translated text can meet the standard of reliability. The TT stresses the promptness of service and gives the impression of "it is only for you", which are highly valued in western cultures. On the other hand, both the ST and TT are intratextually coherent and go in accordance with the cultural background and cognitive process of their target readers. In other words, both are qualified in functioning as an agitating advertisement. Therefore, the functional adaptation can be acceptable in functional translation. In this example, the TT adapted the content in accordance with the familiarity degree of the target readers with the Chinese food culture.

Chapter 5   Loss of Function and Limits of Translatability in Advertising Translation

As has been mentioned in the previous chapters, Chinese and English do not belong to the same language family and cultural system. The cognate equivalence cannot be easily reached. Though functionalist approach to advertising translation allows adaptation in many levels, such as semantic, syntactic and pragmatic, the loss of function, that is to say, the impossibility of achieving approximately the same function is still inevitable in many cases. It has to be admitted that there are still some elements which are substantially untranslatable. In this chapter, the author of this book intends to show tentatively the limits of translatability in the sense of the loss of function, which occurs frequently in advertising translation especially between English and Chinese. Of course, the intention is not to criticize it as a weak point. Instead, it is more of an objective description than of criticism. The term untranslatability rather than limits of translatability is preferred by many theorists. According to Catford, untranslatability falls into two categories: the linguistic untranslatability and cultural untranslatability. "Translation fails—or untranslatability occurs when it is impossible to build functionally relevant features of the situation into the contextual meaning of TL text. " (Catford, 1995: 94) Actually, I would rather use the phrase "limit of translatability", for I personally think the term "untranslatability" is quite misleading. As is known to all, translation proper is a form of intercultural communication. Because of that, the approval of untranslatability between different languages means denying the possibility of human communication, which violates the reality that communication between different cultures does exist extensively and tend to be increasingly frequent in modern society, while the term limits of translatability not only affirms the possibility of intercultural communication but also the actual existence of the inevitable loss of meaning and function to some degree in some cases because of the differences between languages and cultures. By limits of translatability in advertising translation, this book means that the semantic loss or replacement in the process of translation because of the functionally relevant features in the SL leads undoubtedly to the discount of advertising effect of TT and thus the reduction or belittlement of the persuasive function of the TT as an advertisement in the TC.

5. 1   Limits of Linguistic Translatability in Advertising Translation

In the limits of linguistic translatability, the functionally relevant features include some which are in fact formal features of the language of the SL text. If the TL has no formally corresponding feature, the text, or the item, is relatively untranslatable. Limits of linguistic translatability occur typically in cases when an ambiguity peculiar to the ST is a functionally relevant feature, for example, in SL puns. This is particularly the case in advertising translation. Some tricky advertisers utilize the concise and humorous feature of puns to advertise their products tactfully. However, punning advertisements cannot always be satisfactorily translated. Even when the translation skopos has been adequately realized in the TT, the loss in many respects is always inevitable.

5. 1. 1   Concerning Puns

Pun is a figure of speech depending upon a similarity of sound and a disparity of meaning. The translation of puns has long been a big headache for translators, due to the duality of meaning caused by phonetic or formal similarity. In most cases, the ambiguity of meaning is not difficult to distinguish in context. However, if the ambiguity is created intentionally by the author to create certain effect in certain situation, as is the case in most advertisements, it is virtually impossible to translate. The book will elaborate this point by adopting the concepts of shared exponence and polysemy put forward by Catford.

①Shared exponence

Shared exponence means those cases where two or more distinct lexical or grammatical items are expounded in one and the same phonological or graphological form. The advertisers sometimes utilize this characteristic of shared exponence for a better advertising effect. For example:

(12) ST: The driver is safer when the road is dry;
The road is safer when the driver is dry.
TT: 路面干燥，司机安全；
司机清醒，道路安全。（裕晶，陈寅涛，2000: 28）
(13) ST: I'm more satisfied.
Ask for More.
TT: 摩尔香烟，我更满意。
再来一支，还吸摩尔。（肖新英，2021: 40）

Example (12) is a piece of road security slogan, which advocates safe driving. In the ST, "dry" is the graphological shared exponent of two distinctive lexical items in English: one meaning "no water" and the other, "not drink". The two "dry" s in the ST are effective in arousing curiosity of the addressee and inducing them to digest the connotative meaning carefully. However, for lack of corresponding lexical shared exponence in the TL, the literal translation contributes inevitably to the loss of impressive effect and more importantly, does not accord with the logic of Chinese people and the cognitive process of them due to the lack of coherence between the two parts of TT. In Example (13), the ST is witty enough to adopt the puns, which are shared exponence of the adverb "more" and the noun trademark "More". By the grammatical and semantic function of the adverb "more", the More cigarette shows its superior quality to others. The translator attempts to use the method of "unpacking" by making explicit what is structurally implicit in the ST step by step. From the functionalist point of view, this can be seen as a successful translation to some extent for the translation skopos can be achieved if aided by some extra-language elements such as a romantic picture and beautiful music. However, it makes no sense in the respect of the original punning effect. In this example, the punning atmosphere is itself a functionally relevant feature of the SL and there is no such a corresponding phenomenon in the TL. Therefore, the belittlement of communicative function will inevitably occur.

②Polysemy

Polysemy refers to the case of one item having a wide or general contextual meaning, covering a wide range of specific situational features(Catford J. C.,1965: 96). Normally, the context shows which part of the total contextual meaning is functionally relevant and translation presents no problem. But for some cases, as frequently appear in advertisement; the polysemy itself is the functionally relevant feature. That's to say, the polysemy effect is created intentionally by the advertiser. In these cases, it is virtually impossible to avoid the loss of persuasive function of advertising more or less. The following is an example of polysemy:

(14) ST: Better late than the late.
TT1: 迟到总比丧命好。
TT2: 宁迟一时，不辞一世。

The term "late" has more than one contextual meaning—the opposite meaning to "early" as in the first part of the ST and the euphemism for "the dead" as in the second part of the ST. In English cultural background, it is not difficult to distinguish the contextual meaning. However, it is difficult to reproduce the punning effect by a corresponding polysemy in Chinese. TT1, a literal translation by removing the rhetoric punning use, sounds more like a joking utterance than a warning notice. TT2, which shows some advantages compared with the first one, can be regarded as an example of functional translation since it can function as a vocative warning notice though some efforts have to be made for a proper understanding. However, the humorous and affecting function is reduced greatly due to the absence of a corresponding shared exponence or polysemy in Chinese language. In this regard, an adequately functional translation may inevitably lose something that is important to the full realization of the intended function of an advertisement.

5. 1. 2   Concerning Coinages

In order to make their advertisement humorous and attractive, some witty advertisers sometimes coin words and phrases after some well-known ones so that the readers will be curious at their products. However, it always produces difficulty in translating, since the words and phrases they coined after usually belong uniquely to the SL culture. The following is a piece of advertisement of a store selling eggs:

(15) ST: We know Eggsactly how to sell eggs.

TT: 不图虚名，蛋求无过。（肖新英，2021: 42）

(16) ST: What could be delisher than fisher?

TT: 还有什么比钓鱼更有味？

（张旖璇，刘艳，2021: 24）

In Example (15), the word "Eggsactly", coined after "exactly", embodies the expert capacity of the shopkeeper in egg-selling business and also indicates the type of business is acquainted with the customers. The TT, also incorporating a coinage broadly accepted in Chinese (但求无过), can function similarly with the ST. However, the original intention of showing the seller's acquaintance with the egg-selling business has been lost. What is emphasized is the high quality of the eggs sold. The semantic replacement is considerable in this so-called functional translation. In Example (16), the word "delisher" originates from the word "delicious". Such a treatment, together with the word "fisher" coming next, creates allusive effect and adds to the rhythm. The TT, though literally conveyed the exact meaning of the ST, reads insipid, thus discounting the humorous and rhythm effect of the ST. In the above examples, the effectiveness and expressiveness, thus persuasiveness of the original advertising texts fade or even disappear in the translated texts from advertising point of view due to the lack of a corresponding coinage in Chinese that can function satisfactorily in this circumstance.

Chinese advertisers also frequently coin after some well-known idioms and phrases, such as "大石（事）化小，小石（事）化了", "月季花油，看看（遥遥）领先". In these cases, the coinages themselves are functionally relevant features and actually untranslatable in a strict sense.

In the previous part of this chapter, the loss of function and the limits of translatability are mainly caused by unique linguistically functionally relevant features in the SL and are called by Catford and Newmark "linguistic untranslatability". In the following part, the limits of translatability caused mainly by culturally relevant features will be discussed.

5. 2   Limits of Cultural Translatability in AdvertisingTranslation

As has been discussed in previous chapters, cultural elements play an important role in advertising translation. Some elements belong uniquely to a certain culture and can function effectively so far as advertising effects are concerned. When these elements become functionally relevant features in translation, the translation is substantially impossible due to the lack of corresponding cultural elements in the target language. This type of limits of translatability is usually less absolute than the limits of linguistic translatability. There are many cultural elements that may affect the effectiveness of the translated texts. Some aspects will be dealt with in this part as examples.

5. 2. 1 Concerning Idioms

Idioms are the phrases or sentences whose meaning is not clear from the meaning of its individual words and which must be learnt as a whole unit. They usually belong uniquely to a certain culture and can not be easily understood by non-native speakers. When the idioms are the functionally relevant features of the source texts, the loss of advertising function to some degree are substantially inevitable. For example:

(17) ST: You will go nuts for the nuts you get in Nux.
TT: 纳克斯坚果让你爱不释口。

In the ST, "go nuts" is an idiom which means "go crazy" in English culture. The translator attempts to compensate the cultural blank by an adapted Chinese idiom ("爱不释口" from "爱不释手"). However, there is still some distance from "爱不释口" to "go crazy". Moreover, the punning effect of the original sentence is nearly completely lost. If translated literally, such a sentence, which goes naturally in English reader's minds, makes no sense at all to most Chinese readers. To bridge the cultural gap that results in the limits of translatability, there is still a long way to go.

5. 2. 2   Concerning Literary Works

Some literary works are particularly influential to the culture from which they originate. Some are worldly influential. In these cases, the limits of translatability caused by these literary works will still be considerable in translation, though reduced to some degree. The following is an example in this respect. The famous British newspaper "The Thames" has an advertising slogan, which incorporates the name of world-known literary work "Pride and Prejudice": "We take no pride in prejudice. " Someone translated it into "对于您的傲慢，我们没有偏见". "Pride and Prejudice" is a famous novel written by the Britain woman writer Jane Austin. The book has invasive influence upon most English people, so the press quoted the book's name to build up its image of justice in a tactful way. However, to ordinary Chinese people, the book name does not sound so loud. A large proportion of the people knows nothing about it at all. Consequently, the translated version makes no sense to them. Some may even think it an insult due to the term "傲慢", which is often negatively used in meaning. The translated version still seems awkward for it is not an integral part of Chinese culture.

5.3　Translatability and Untranslatability: A Dynamic Continuum

Translatability and untranslatability remain, rather than a clear-cut and static dichotomy, a dynamic and multidimensional cline from absolute untranslatability to absolute translatability which actually serves merely two assumed extreme states in the continuum. Any SL texts and items are more or less translatable rather than absolutely translatable or untranslatable because of the objective existence of linguistic commonality and cultural humanity and the flood of continuous worldwide cultural communication and ferment (Zhou Xiaohan, 2020: 30).

With the opening up to the outside world and the fast development of globalization, people become increasingly ready to accept foreign linguistic and cultural elements. Nowadays, ordinary Chinese people can easily accept some English terms that had to be translated by meaning years ago with nearly no barriers. For example, "crocodile's tears" and "armed to the teeth" had to be translated into "猫哭耗子——假慈悲" and "全副武装", or the like.However, nowadays most people accept the literal translation "鳄鱼的眼泪" and "武装到牙齿". It is the result of continuous cultural contact and interchange.

In comparison, linguistic untranslatability is more absolute than cultural untranslatability. However, it is still not completely untranslatable. For example, on the body of a teakettle for export, there is a circle of Chinese characters read as follows.

(18) ST:　　　2 以

　　　1 可　　　清 3

　　　5 也　　　心 4

This magic circle attributes to the multifunctional feature of Chinese characters and the semantic and syntactic shifts of them. Different punctuation can lead to different interpretation of the circle. Read clockwise, the circle has five interpretations with meaning nuances. (i) It can refresh your heart. (可以清心也); (ii) It can also refresh your heart. (以清心也可); (iii) Refreshing heart is also one of its functions. (清心也可以); (iv) Your heart can also be refreshed. (心也可以清); (v) Similar to（也可以清心）. The underlined parts are stressed in each version. This magic circle can help the customer appreciate Chinese tea culture while enjoying the tea. But this stylistically attractive feature can hardly find an equivalent in English due to the uniqueness of ancient Chinese language, so it has been labeled as a typical example of untransltability for many years in the field of translation until 1998 when Pro. Zuo's postgraduates made an attempt at the transformation of the magic circle as follows (Zhou Xiaohan, 2020: 47).

TT: Tea (brings a) reposeful mind.

(A) reposeful mind (comes from) tea.

Mind, (enjoying) tea (is) reposeful.

（周晓寒，2020: 30）

The TT adds the omitted "tea" and leaves out "ke", "yi" and "ye" in the ST to retain the circulating readability. Creation to this degree is acceptable from functionalist perspective. Though not perfect, it remains a bold attempt at breaking away from the untranslatability and has proved the translatability to a large degree. Judging from the functionalist theories, it can be regarded as legitimate to some extent.

From this example, we can see that the untranslatability is not an absolute definition. It can be said that there is a continuum between completely translatable and completely untranslatable. The scale will move in the positive direction along with the improvement of translation theories and the global cultural exchange and ferment.

From the above discussion in this chapter, it is seen that functionalist translation theories are not omnipotent. In many cases, the limits of translatability will inevitably occur as a result of unique linguistic or cultural functionally relevant features in the source languages. Even when the functionalist approach has been successfully carried out, some losses in semantic or formal sense will occur inevitably in many cases. However, the concept of untranslatability is not absolute. With the deepening of international interaction and the improvement of translation theories, the translatability will be enlarged little by little.

Chapter 6　Conclusion

In this part, the author will conclude the research through a summary of the major findings and the limitations of the present study as well as the suggestions for future research.

As a text for special purpose, the advertisement has its unique stylistic characteristics, which determines that advertising translation should have its own principles, criteria and approaches. And it should be studied in terms of not only surface structure but also intrinsic mechanism. Due to the nature of advertising that distinguishes itself from other types of texts such as literature and technical texts, advertising translation, which is affected by many parameters, internal and external ones, means not just a SL-TL linguistic operation, but often an adaptation process according to the factors of the target culture. However, the traditional equivalence-based linguistic approach to translation has gradually showed its defects and incompetence when guiding advertising translation. Having made a breakthrough in translation field which had been dominated by equivalence theories for quite a long time, German functionalist theories have proved to be effective and competent enough to work as theoretical basis of advertising translation in that they have dethroned the foremost position of the ST in the translation process and confirmed the primary importance of the translation skopos, that is, the expected function of the TT and set up functional adequacy as new assessment criterion of translation validity rather than equivalent effect standard by traditional equivalence-based theories. Therefore, functionalist theories provide the present study with a sound theoretical framework. Accordingly, this book holds that the target-language-culture oriented strategy should be taken as the basic strategy of advertising translation and a variety of specific methods, especially addition, abridgement and rewriting which are excluded from the domain of translation studies by traditional equivalence-based translation theories, should be employed flexibly in order to produce an effective, operative text for the target market. Of course, the predominance of certain strategy and methods is also prone to change depending on the economic and cultural environment especially with the acceleration of global cultural communication and ferment. But no translation theory can summarize all the translation situations. So does functionalist approach to translation. It can only be applied in some text types whose translation allows adaptation to some extent. Besides, it fails to solve the problem of the loss in semantic, formal and consequently communicative function as elaborated in Chapter 5.

The author of this book has expected to provide a comprehensive analysis of advertising and its translation. However, in trying to grasp all points, she must have lost some.

Firstly, the analysis may have covered a wide range of topics, but they are not thorough and profound enough. Some of the discussions still need improvement. For example, the probing into the limits of translatability seems shallow and scattered, lacking in deep and systematic theoretical exploration.

Secondly, the examples cited in the research are rather limited and may not be representative enough. Therefore, the study and analysis are not very objective and exhaustive. Things will get better if there is an established parallel corpus of paired advertisements.

On the basis of the findings and limitations of this book, the author attempts to give some recommendations for further research in the field of advertising translation.

Changing the media researched (for example, television, newspaper, billboard or Internet advertising) which would paint a fuller picture of the genre.

Paying attention to the transfer of non-verbal signs, such as light, sound and motion, etc. which play an increasingly important even indispensable part in international advertising.

Concentrating on specific product categories (such as cosmetics and cars) to ascertain whether translation strategies and methods are product bound.

Investigating how translated advertisements are received and understood by the target audience and what differences exist between the reception of translated advertisements and those originally written ones by incorporating concepts of cognitive psychology.

References

[1] Austin J. L. *How to Do things with Words*[M]. Oxford: Clarendon Press, 1962.

[2] Catford, J. C. *A Linguistic Theory of Translation: An Essay on Applied Linguistics* [M]. London: Oxford University Press, 1965.

[3] Chesterman, A. *Memes of Translation: The Spread of Ideas in Translation Theory*[M]. Amsterdam/Philadelphia: John Benjamins Publishing Company, 1997.

[4] Guidere, M. *Translating Ads* [M]. Paris: Harmattan, 2000.

[5] Hurbin, P. *Peut-on traduire la langue de la publicite*[J]. Babel, 1972, 18(3): 24-32.

[6] Mark, S., Moira, C. *Dictionary of Translation Studies* [M] . Shanghai: Shanghai Foreign Language Education Press, 2004.

[7] Mueller, B. *International Advertising: Communicating Across Cultures*[M]. Dalian: Dongbei University of Finance& Economics, 1998.

[8] Munday, J. *Introducing Translation Studies: Theory and*

Applications [M]. London: Routledge, 2001.

[9] Newmark, P. *Approaches to Translation*[M]. Shanghai: Shanghai Foreign Language Education Press, 2001.

[10] Newmark, P. *A Textbook of Translation*[M].Shanghai: Shanghai Foreign Language Education Press, 2002.

[11] Nida, E. A. *Language and Culture—Contexts in Translating*[M]. Shanghai: Shanghai Foreign Language Education Press, 2001.

[12] Nord, C. *Text Analysis in Translation*[M]. Amsterdam: Brill Academic Publishers, 2006.

[13] Nord, C. *Translating as a Purposeful Activity—Functionalist Approaches Explained*[M]. Shanghai: Shanghai Foreign Language Education Press, 2001.

[14] Reiss, K. Text Types, *Translation Types and Translation Assessment*[M]. trans. by Chesterman, A. Nairobi: East African Scholars Press, 2020.

[15] Seguinot, C. Translation and Advertising: Going Global[C]// Schaffner, C., Kelly-Holmes, H. (eds.) *Cultural Functions of Translation*. Clevedon: Multilingual Matters, 1994.

[16] Smith, V. & C. Klein-Braley. *Advertising——A Five-stage Strategy for Translation*[M]// C. Nord, et al. *Translation as Intercultural Communication*. Amsterdam: Benjamins, 1997: 174-184.

[17] Snell-Hornby, M. *Translation Studies—An Integrated Approach*[M]. Shanghai: Shanghai Foreign Language

Education Press, 2001.

[18] Tanaka K. *Advertising Language: A Pragmatic Approach to Advertisements in Britain and Japan*[M]. London/New York: Routledge, 1994.

[19] 闲思明. 数字传播时代广告语言的修辞艺术 [J]. 中国广告, 2021（08）：75-78.

[20] 蔡力坚. 把适当的词放在适当的地方 [J]. 中国翻译, 2021（05）：183-186.

[21] 蔡力坚. 中文特有并列结构的英译处理 [J]. 中国翻译, 2021（04）：158-165.

[22] 陈诺梅，黄丽花，周春帆，等. 论广告语言的创新性与审美性传媒论坛，2020（20）：117-118.

[23] 丁俊杰，康瑾. 现代广告通论 [M]. 第四版. 北京：中国传媒大学出版社，2019.

[24] 杜爽爽. 浅析广告翻译的现状（中英互译）与翻译策略 [J]. 校园英语，2020（02）：249.

[25] 郭大民. 英语广告的语言特色及翻译技巧探思 [J]. 学园，2020（32）：102-104.

[26] 郭建中. 翻译中的文化因素：异化与归化 [J]. 外国语, 1998（02）：12-18.

[27] 郭建中. 文化与翻译 [C]. 北京：中国对外翻译出版公司, 2000.

[28] 韩玮. 跨文化交际视角下的英汉翻译归化与异化 [J]. 校园英语，2021（37）：248-249.

[29] 韩旭，李延林. 广告翻译的跨文化视角 [J]. 中国科技翻译，2017（02）：28-30, 43.

[30] 何青南. 论广告语言中的双关辞格 [J]. 参花（下）, 2020
（11）：36-37.

[31] 季鹏程. 广告语言的象似性研究 [J]. 海外英语, 2020（13）：
231-232.

[32] 荆艳君. 商标翻译原则和方法探究 [J]. 大陆桥视野,
2021（12）：81-82.

[33] 贾文波. 广告口号对外翻译：顺应译语体裁规约 [J]. 花炮
科技与市场, 2018（04）：130.

[34] 宓庆. 文体与翻译 [M]. 北京：中国对外翻译出版公司,
1998.

[35] 宓庆. 文化翻译论纲 [M]. 武汉：湖北教育出版社, 1999.

[36] 宓庆. 当代翻译理论 [M]. 北京：中国对外翻译出版公司,
1999.

[37] 刘帅, 王丹彤. 浅析几种常见应用文体的翻译策略 [J]. 作
家天地, 2021（22）：54-55.

[38] 刘婷. 言语行为理论下的广告语言 [J]. 现代交际, 2021
（15）：133-135.

[39] 刘潇, 刘著妍. 汉语广告英译的语用等效翻译 [J]. 开封教
育学院学报, 2018（08）：77-78.

[40] 卢怡阳. 功能视角下的广告语翻译 [J]. 知识文库, 2021
（01）：15-17.

[41] 王津津. 广告翻译中对语用学理论的使用 [J]. 现代职业教
育, 2018（20）：229.

[42] 王京平, 杨帆. 德国功能翻译理论学者克里斯蒂安娜·诺
德采访录 [J]. 德语人文研究, 2021（01）：43-46.

[43] 王小琼. 关注过程：建构"以实践为导向"的应用文体翻

译课堂 [J]. 山西能源学院学报，2020（06）：41-43.

[44] 苏竹筠. 翻译研究的跨学科性及其边界拓展——吕克·范·多斯拉尔教授访谈录 [J]. 中国翻译，2021（04）：101-105.

[45] 吴玥迪. 结合广告的功能目的分析其翻译策略 [J]. 海外英语. 2020（24）：84-85.

[46] 肖新英. 英汉广告语篇翻译的"三生三适" [J]. 中国科技翻译，2021（04）：40-42.

[47] 肖新英. 论广告翻译中的生态限制因子 [J]. 中国科技翻译，2018（03）：25-27.

[48] 谢天振. 翻译研究新视野 [M]. 青岛：青岛出版社，2003.

[49] 徐婷婷. 从目的论看商业广告翻译与策略（英文）[J]. 中阿科技论坛（中英文), 2021（08）：208-210.

[50] 严琦. 跨文化视角下商务英语广告的语言特点与翻译策略分析 [J]. 现代英语，2021（23）：69-71.

[51] 杨仕芬. 广告中英语修辞的运用和翻译策略 [J]. 校园英语，2020（23）：240-241.

[52] 杨自俭. 英汉语比较与翻译 3 [C]. 上海：上海外语教育出版社，2000.

[53] 张道振. 从传统走向现代——论描写翻译批评的现代理念、方法和任务 [J]. 外国语（上海外国语大学学报），2021（06）：94-102.

[54] 余静. 规范冲突中的翻译行为模式研究 [J]. 外国语（上海外国语大学学报), 2020（04）：92-99.

[55] 张东东. 目的论视角下的商务英语广告翻译浅析 [J]. 海外英语，2020（24）：97-98.

[56] 张海荣. 化妆品广告语段中的语言策略研究 [D]. 武汉：华中师范大学，2020.

[57] 张举栋. 从语言哲学角度观照"翻译"——与刘宓庆教授谈"究竟何谓'翻译'"[J]. 中国翻译，2021（05）：98-104.

[58] 张旖璇，刘艳. 从关联理论分析广告双关语的翻译 [J]. 汉字文化，2021（18）：35-38.

[59] 张芸芸. 行为与交际：功能派理论的发展与翻译概念的革新——浅谈贾斯塔·霍尔兹-曼塔利和她的翻译行为理论 [J]. 海外英语，2020（18）：82-83.

[60] 赵慧. 功能对等理论视角下的中英商务广告翻译研究 [J]. 校园英语，2021（11）：255-256.

[61] 赵滢滢. 描述翻译学视角下的翻译策略研究——以《日耳曼人》（节选）为例 [D]. 成都：四川外国语大学，2019.

[62] 周晓寒. 文化不可译性与补偿策略研究——以《射雕英雄传》英译本为例 [D]. 福州：福建师范大学，2020.

[63] 朱小华. 语用学视野下的广告语翻译研究 [J]. 校园英语，2017（40）：217-218.

Acknowledgements

I hereby would like to express my heart-felt thanks and gratitude to many people, who have contributed to the completion of this book. Firstly, I would like to extend my sincere thanks to Prof. Shu Qizhi, my respected teacher and supervisor, for her strict supervision, warm-hearted encouragement, and valuable suggestions in the process of my writing this book.

I also would like to thank all the professors in the College of Foreign Languages of Xiangtan University, for their illuminating lectures on approaches to translation, on translation of writing for special purposes, on stylistics and on Chinese-English cultures, etc, which have inspired me to explore deeper into the field the book is concerned with.

In addition, I am grateful to all the respondents for their generous assistance with the two surveys which constitute an important part of the book.

At last, my thanks go to my family members for their love, patience and support.

Appendix A: Related Publications & Research

1. Academic Papers Published（已发论文）

[1] Dong, Yan. The Construction of International Higher Education Zone of Guangdong-Hong Kong-Macao Greater Bay Area: The Status Quo and Strategies[J]. *Modern Management Forum*, 2023(1): 23-25.

[2] Dong, Yan. The Assignment Design for Business English Writing from the Perspective of Outcome Based Education: a Case Study[J]. *International Education and Development*, 2022(6): 59-65 .

[3] Dong, Yan. Application of Production-Oriented Approach in College English Teaching[J]. *International Education and Development*, 2022(4): 53-57.

[4] Dong, Yan. Study on Translation Strategies of Intangible Cultural Heritage from the Perspective of Ecotranslat-

ol[J]. *Research on Literary and Art Development*, 2022(3): 8-11.

[5] Dong, Yan. Research on the Internationalization Strategy of Higher Education in Guangdong-Hong Kong-Macao Greater Bay Area[J].*International Education And Development*, 2021(8): 109-114.

[6] 董岩. 遵循教育发展规律、转变高校办学理念——评《高等教育国际化：动因、策略及国别研究》[J]. 山西财经大学学报，2022（8）：130.

[7] 董岩. 常用商务英语口语中与"水"相关的英语表达探析[J]. 给水排水，2022（4）：30-31.

[8] 董岩. 跨文化商务谈判中文化差异对英语翻译的影响研究——评《商务英语谈判》[J]. 科技管理研究，2021（8）：220.

[9] 董岩. 中欧文化语境与交际风格的跨文化解读[J]. 海外英语，2021（7）：192-193.

[10] 董岩. 旅游英语教学中汉语言文化导入问题探究[J]. 教学与研究，2021（4）：248.

[11] 董岩. 湖南非物质文化遗产新媒体外宣现状与对策研究[J]. 文化创新比较研究，2021（4）：132-135.

[12] 董岩. 新时代高校立德树人研究述评与展望[J]. 文化创新比较研究，2021（4）：1-4.

[13] 董岩. 大学英语"课程思政"教学探索与实践研究现状述评[J]. 文教资料，2021（3）：130-131.

[14] 董岩，唐贡如. 广告口号翻译浅探[J]. 文教资料，2020（10）：46-47.

[15] 董岩．基于英语学科核心素养的产出导向型大学英语教学研究 [J]．教育学文摘，2020（7）：249.

[16] 董岩．"产出导向法"国内外研究述评 [J]．教学与研究，2020（7）：270.

[17] 董岩．英语学科核心素养研究述评 [J]．科学大众．科学教育，2020（4）：164.

[18] 董岩．元认知学习策略与大学英语网络自主学习 [J]．求知导刊，2018（7）：98.

[19] 董岩．大学英语网络自主学习效率低下现象剖析 [J]．当代教育理论与实践，2014（11）：108-109.

[20] 董岩,林小平．人本主义学习理论对独立学院大学英语教学的启示 [J]．当代教育理论与实践，2012（12）：113-114.

[21] 董岩．外宣资料：交际功能及其编译 [J]．内蒙古农业大学学报（社会科学版），2011（6）：355-356.

[22] 董岩．建构主义翻译研究范式解读 [J]．吉林工程技术师范学院学报，2011（10）：42-44.

[23] 董岩．中西不中听信息的交际风格透视 [J]．吉林工程技术师范学院学报，2010（4）：44-46.

[24] 董岩．权势距离与不中听信息的交际风格的跨文化透视 [J]．内蒙古农业大学学报（社会科学版），2010（4）：193-194.

[25] 董岩,张雪珠．元认知策略与英语词汇自主学习 [J]．河北理工大学学报，2010（4）：121-122.

[26] 董岩．仿拟的世界——英汉拟声词的对比研究 [J]．牡丹江教育学院学报，2010（1）：27-28.

[27] 董岩．广告语篇翻译的功能性策略与方法 [J]．内蒙古农

业大学学报（社会科学版），2009（5）：349-351.

[28] 董岩. 功能派译论视角下的商标翻译 [J]. 陇东学院学报，2009（5）：66-68.

[29] 董岩. 旅游英语教学中的文化素质教育问题新思考 [J]. 吉林工程技术师范学院学报，2009（9）：53-55.

[30] 董岩. 大学英语教学中的文化导入问题新思考 [J]. 河北理工大学学报，2009（2）：161-162.

[31] 董岩. 广告翻译的可译性限度研究——德国功能派译论的视角 [J]. 内蒙古农业大学学报（社会科学版），2008（3）：325-327.

[32] 董岩. 广告翻译的功能性策略和方法 [J]. 齐齐哈尔大学学报（社会科学版），2008（1）：160-162.

[33] 董岩. 汉英亲属称谓语的文化隐喻及其翻译 [J]. 琼州大学学报，2007（1）：77-79.

[34] 董岩. 介词 over 的意象图式及其空间概念隐喻的多维思考 [J]. 吉林化工学院学报，2006（6）：68-71.

[35] 董岩. 汉英请求语篇模式与文化思维方式 [J]. 河西学院学报，2006（4）：97-100.

[36] 董岩. 汉英亲属称谓语的文化隐喻 [J]. 湘潭师范学院学报（社会科学版），2006（2）：98-100.

[37] 董岩，舒奇志. 英汉称谓语的文化隐喻 [J]. 湘潭师范学院学报（社会科学版），2005（2）：128-132.

[38] 董岩，舒奇志. 从"不中听"信息的传递看中西交际风格的文化差异 [J]. 忻州师范学院学报，2004（6）：95-99.

[39] 董岩. "不中听"信息的交际风格的文化差异初探 [J]. 怀化学院学报，2004（6）：30-32.

2. Monograph（专著）

[1] 董岩. 多维视角下的英语语言文化研究 [M]. 哈尔滨：东北林业大学出版社，2021.

3. Research Programs（研究项目）

[1] 2022 年度广东省哲学社会科学"十四五"规划学科共建课题《新媒体语境下广东非物质文化遗产翻译与国际传播之现状与策略研究》（省级，编号：GD22XWY07）（主持人：董岩）

[2] 2022 年度广东省高等教育学会"十四五"规划高等教育研究课题《基于三角协调模型的粤港澳大湾区国际高等教育示范区建设策略研究》（市级，编号：22GYB75）（主持人：董岩）

[3] 2022 年度广东省广州市哲学社会科学"十四五"规划课题《"讲好中国故事"背景下广府文化国际传播现状与策略研究》（市级，编号：2021GZGJ238）（主持人：董岩）

[4] 2021 年度广东省教育科学规划课题《粤港澳大湾区国际高等教育示范区建设现状与策略研究》（省级，编号：2021GXJK127）（主持人：董岩）

[5] 2021 年度教育部外语教指委教改课题《基于"产出导向法"的商务英语口语课程思政混合教学模式研究》（部级，编号：WYJZW-2021-2058）（主持人：董岩）

[6] 2021 年度广东农工商职业技术学院教材建设项目《高职院校外语类专业课程思政案例精析及教学实施》（校级，编号：粤农工商职院 [2021]237 号第 25 项）（主持人：董岩）

[7] 2021 年度广东农工商职业技术学院"课程思政"研究项目《基于"成果导向"的剑桥商务英语课程思政混合教学模式研究与实践》（校级，编号：XJSZZD202101）（主持人：董岩）

[8] 2020 年湖南省普通高等学校教学改革研究项目《基于"产出导向法"的大学英语"课程思政"教学探索与实践》（省级，编号：HNJG-2020-0528，2020-2023）（主持人：董岩）

[9] 2020 年度湖南省社会科学成果评审委员会课题《"一带一路"背景下湖南非物质文化遗产新媒体外宣现状与对策研究（省级，编号：XSP20YBZ180）（主持人：董岩）

[10] 2019 年度湖南省社科基金外语科研联合项目《"一带一路"背景下湖南非物质文化遗产网络外宣翻译问题与对策研究》（省级，编号：19WLH15）（主持人：董岩）

[11] 2019 年度湖南省教育科学"十三五"规划课题《基于英语学科核心素养的产出导向型大学英语教学模式研究》（省级，编号：XJK19CGD019）（主持人：董岩）

[12] 2011 年湖南省普通高等学校教学改革研究项目《独立学院大学英语教学模式改革实践研究》（省级，编号：湘教通 [2011]315 号第 226 项）。（主持人：董岩）

[13] 2009 年度湖南省教育厅科学研究项目《基于建构主义的外宣翻译研究》（省级，编号：09C420）（主持人：董岩）

[14] 2009 年度湖南科技大学科研课题《"不中听"信息的传递模式及交际风格的跨文化研究》（校级，编号：08K005）（主持人：董岩）

Appendix B: The Questionnaire

No.1 This is an ad for a brand of pencil made in Shanghai, China.

Version A:

Shanghai Zhonghua pencils:

First-class quality, smooth writing and elegant design.

Version B:

Shanghai Zhonghua pencils:

Super quality smoothes your writing;

Brilliant design reveals your taste.

Version C:

Shanghai China pencils:

Super quality, smooth writing and smart design.

Question:

Which one do you think is the best?

    A. Version A.   B. Version B.   C. Version C.

No. 2 This is an ad for Pudong Shangri-La Hotel.

Version A:

Pudong Shanghai is the 14th hotel opened by Shangri-La Hotel Management Group in China. The hotel has 612 guest rooms, each covering more than 39 square meters. The guest rooms fall into six categories—standard rooms, luxury rooms, luxury rooms with beautiful view of the Bund, luxury chambers, suites and one presidential suite. The hotel is noted for its amazing, unique dishes and comprehensive entertainment facilities. Its Xianggong Chinese Restaurant has Guangdong cuisine, Shanghai delicacies, and local snacks. The restaurant has earned high appreciation from customers for its excellent service and delicious food.

Version B:

The award-winning Pudong Shangri-La Hotel is located in the Lujiazui Finance and Trade Zone of Shanghai. It enjoys easy access to both Hongqiao and Pudong international airports and is also close to the subway connecting Pudong (East Shanghai) to Puxi (West Shanghai). Prominently sited along the famous Huangpu River, the Hotel has breathtaking views of Shanghai's legendary riverfront—the Bund and the Orient Pearl TV Tower. Its 606 rooms are the most spacious in the city and are complemented by an extensive range of restaurants, lounges and bars.

Question:

Obviously, the information contained in Version A and Version B is quite different. Which one do you think provides the more important, useful and necessary information from the consumers' perspective?

A. Version A.　　B. Version B.　　C. None.

3. The language of which version is more natural and easier to understand in your culture?

A. Version A.　　B. Version B.　　C. None.

4. Supposing you were a consumer, which version would most probably impress you and persuade you to take action?

A. Version A.　　B. Version B.　　C. None.

The Chinese original text attached.

No.1　上海中华铅笔：品质优良，书写润滑，美观大方。

No.2　上海浦东香格里拉饭店是香格里拉集团在中国开设的第 14 家饭店。饭店包括 612 间客房，每间客房面积超过 39 平方米。客房共分六类：标准间、豪华间、可观赏外滩美丽景色的豪华间、豪华单人间、豪华套房及一套总统套房。上海浦东香格里拉饭店以特色美味和综合娱乐设施而著名。在香宫中国餐厅可以品尝到广东风味、上海风味及地方小吃。香宫餐厅因其优质服务和美味可口的饭菜在客人中享有盛誉。

Appendix C: Informative Chinese Abstract

功能派译论视角下的英汉广告互译

　　本书的研究主要探讨功能派译论在英汉广告互译中的应用，尝试提供广告翻译的可行性策略并探讨广告翻译中的可译性限度问题，从而在广告翻译的大量实践与尚不充分的理论研究之间架起一座桥梁。此研究采用以定性研究为主、定量研究为辅的方法，定性研究主要采用论证的形式，定量研究采用问卷调查的形式。此外，由于篇幅所限，本书主要探讨商业广告的翻译，且仅限于广告文本中言语符号的转换，公益广告的翻译、广告文本中的非言语符号的传译等问题不在本书探讨的范围。

　　根据美国营销协会的定义，广告是指由可确认的广告主，对其观念、商品或服务所作之任何方式付款的非人员性的陈述与推广。现代社会，广告已渗透到社会的各个角落，逐渐成为人们日常生活中的一个重要组成部分，广告及其翻译在经济全球化中的作用日益凸显。作为翻译学的一个分支，广告翻译有着不同于文学翻译的内在特点和规律，因而有必要对其进行系统的研究。

广告文体是一种实用性文体。任何广告都具有两个基本功能：信息功能和劝诱功能，其中，劝诱功能是最根本的功能，信息功能从属于劝诱功能；广告的终极目的是诱导或说服消费者或公众接受某种产品、服务或观点。可见，一则无法说服消费者实施购买行为的广告无疑是失败的广告。同样，在广告翻译中，如果译文无法达到这样的目的就不算是成功的翻译。因此，广告翻译的研究必须把广告的特殊目的、功能与翻译理论有机结合起来。

相对文学翻译研究和佛经翻译研究，广告翻译研究仍是一个年轻的，不成熟的领域。然而，广为推崇的传统等值论（如严复的"信、达、雅"论，奈达的"对等论"）用来指导广告翻译却存在诸多缺陷：（1）等值论将翻译局限于纯语言文本的转换，将非言语符号排除在翻译研究的范畴之外，而非言语符号（如图片、动画、音乐）在国际广告中的地位日益重要甚至不可缺少。（2）由于语言文化的巨大差异，完全的对等或等效无论在理论上还是在实践中均无法实现，有时甚至并不可取。（3）对等论无法解释国际广告实务中的一些特殊现象，如有些产品是完全外向型的，即原语文本只是一些可供译者参考的素材而并非广告，译文是目标文化中的一个独立的广告文本，因而无所谓对等。（4）对等论将一些非传统的翻译方法，如增删、改写等排除在翻译研究之外，而这些方法在广告翻译的实践中普遍存在且非常有效。可见，传统等值论强调译文和原文的对等而忽视译文在目的文化中功能的实现，因而无法适应广告翻译的客观要求。遗憾的是，许多广告翻译研究者仍在对等论的框架下徘徊，许多广告译者仍以对等作为衡量广告译文的标准。

　　作为对传统译论的一个重大突破和重要补充,由费米尔、诺德等学者提出的翻译功能理论为广告翻译的理论研究开辟了一个新的视角。该理论的两大总原则或曰支柱是目的原则和忠诚原则。目的原则是核心,它主张译文预期目的或功能决定整个翻译过程,包括翻译策略和方法的选择。忠诚原则是指译者对原文作者和译文接收者负有道义上的责任,它是诺德为克服极端功能主义的缺陷而提出来的。值得注意的是,"忠诚原则"并不等于传统译论中"忠实"或"对等",前者是就翻译过程中译者与其他参与者之间的社会人际关系而言,而后者就原语文本和译语文本之间的文本关系而言。此外,该理论还包含两个次准则,即强调译文通顺易懂的连贯法则和强调译文忠实于原文的忠实法则。这四大准则的地位并不一致:目的原则和忠诚原则是适用于所有翻译过程的普遍原则,连贯法则和忠实法则是适用于特殊情形的特殊原则;忠实法则从属于连贯法则,二者均从属于目的原则与忠诚原则。

　　功能派译论对广告翻译具有非常有效的指导意义。(1)功能派译论强调目的文本在目标文化中的交际功能的充分实现,因而注重译文收受着(包括其文化层次、世界知识、价值观念、消费习惯等)的角色作用及目标文本交际发生的时间、地点、媒介、社会环境等因素,这与广告文本的特点不谋而合,因为广告的特殊目的和功能决定了广告创作也特别注重目标受众及目标市场的诸多因素。(2)功能派译论引入翻译行为概念,将翻译定义为包括文本转换在内的所有跨文化转换形式，即传统意义上的翻译和翻译行为是两个以跨文化交际为中心的同心圆，只是前者的半径小于后者，这也适应了国际广告中非言语符号的作用日益凸显的客观事实。此外，广告主有时要依赖译者对译语文化的专业知识对文本进行设计或修订，在功能派译论视角下，这种协商、建议均属于翻译行为，因而也是翻译研究的范畴。（3）功能派译论颠覆了原语文本的核心和权威地位，仅将其视为可供译者选择的众多信息源中的一个，这与广告文本的目标受众取向一致。（4）功能派译论赋予译者至关重要的角色作用，他不再是一个隐形的被动的"奴隶"，而是一个显形的有极大主动性和创造性的实体，这与广告创作者的角色作用一致。（5）功能派译论也为一些传统等值论认为非常规的翻译方法，如增删、改写提供了理论支撑，这些方法在广告翻译实践中大量应用而且证明非常有效。（6）从文本类型来看，祈使型文本（如广告）强调文本的潜在交际功能的实现，这与功能派的主要思想相一致，因而祈使型文本需要功能翻译。可见，功能派译论的主要思想与广告文体的特点有诸多契合之处，因而将其作为广告翻译的指导理论具有可行性和科学性。

功能派译论认为，译文预期目的或功能决定整个翻译过程，包括翻译策略和方法的选择。翻译策略是指整个翻译行为和过程的总体导向，而翻译方法则指翻译过程中对语言文字的具体处理办法。一般来说，翻译策略不外乎两种：以原语语言文化为取向的策略（即异化）和以目标语言文化为取向的策略（即归化），前者指译者在翻译中尽量保留原语语言文化的形象和特征，从而在目标文化中显示原语文本的"异质性"，后者指译者努力用目标语言和文化所熟悉和喜好的形象和特征去替换或阐释原语的形象和特征，以迎合目标读者的口味。以原语语言文化为取向的策略顺应了文化交流与融合的趋势，可以使一种文化特有的东西为另一种文化所认识，但译文能否被广泛接受总是有赖于时间和实践的检验，且其可接受性也只能就一定的阶段而言。以目标语言文化为取向的翻译策略可以完全避免这个问题还能充分发挥译文的优势，增强译文的可读性，但它对文化间的差异采取消极回避态度。可见，这两种策略各有其利弊，采取哪种策略应视具体的翻译情形而定。常见的翻译方法有音译，直译，意译，调整（含增加、删减等），重写等，其中音译和直译颇受原语语言文化取向策略的青睐，而意译，调整和重写则多见于以目标语言文化为取向的翻译中。当然，翻译策略和翻译方法之间并没有绝对的必然的对应关系，在翻译策略的指导下如何灵活应用各种翻译方法得靠于译者的文本驾驭能力。

英汉广告在语言表达和文化特质上存在巨大差异。原语文化中产生正面效应的广告如果绝对对等地转换成目的语可能产生零效应甚至负效应。为此，作者进行了一次小规模的问卷调查，旨在测试同一原语广告文本用不同的翻译策略和方法产生的不同广告译文在目标受众中的反映。结果表明，充分考虑目标语言文化和目标受众的特点的译文在目标受众中颇有市场，而保留原语语言文化特质的译文备受冷落，所以广告翻译应以目的语言文化为导向，充分考虑译文在目的语文化中的广告功能的最大限度的实现。广告翻译的大量实例表明，成功的广告译文的译者也都有意无意地遵循以目的语言文化为取向的翻译策略。因此，考虑到广告的特殊目的和功能，本书主张广告翻译应以目的语言文化为导向，灵活应用各种可能的翻译方法（包括音译、直译、意译、增删、改写等）和文本手段，以最大限度地实现广告译文预期的劝诱功能，并从而达到说服消费者实施购买行为的目的。这种功能化的翻译策略和方法适用于完整的广告文本的所有组成部分的翻译，包括商标、广告口号及广告语篇的翻译。

功能派译论并非包医百病的灵丹妙药。由于语言文化的巨大差异，英汉广告互译中有时不可避免地存在不同程度的形式上、意义上的缺失，因而弱化了广告的表达效果和劝诱功能，这就是广告翻译中的可译性限度问题。可译性限度存在于语言和文化两个方面。可译和不可译并非静止的绝对的概念，而是一个动态的多维的连续体，随着语言文化之间的不断交流与融合，原来不可译的可能变得可译，有限度的翻译可能变得充分。

本研究在理论和实践上均有重要意义。迄今为止，对于广告翻译的系统的理论研究尚不充分，广告翻译尚未引起翻译理论家的足够重视，功能派理论打破了传统对等论的束缚，为广告翻译研究开辟了一个新的视角，提供了更加可行和科学的理论根基。在实践上，功能派译论为广告翻译中的一些非常规的翻译方法提供了理论支撑并为广告译文的评价提供了新的标准。对于可译性限度问题的探讨也表明了包括功能派理论在内的任何翻译理论都并非全能。

　　本书的研究只触及广告翻译在某些方面的问题，广告翻译的其他方面，如公益广告的翻译，广告文本中非言语符号的转换、商品类型与翻译策略的关系、广告翻译的认知心理学视角，则需要进行更加广泛而深入的研究。